Chicago

A guide to recent architecture

D1315494

...

Susanna Sirefman

Chicago

A guide to recent architecture

● ● ● **ellipsis KÖNEMANN**

● ● ●

Chicago: a guide to recent architecture

CREATED, EDITED AND DESIGNED BY
Ellipsis London Limited
55 Charlotte Road London EC2A 3QT
E MAIL ...@ellipsis.co.uk
WWW http://www.ellipsis.co.uk/ellipsis
PUBLISHED IN THE UK AND AFRICA BY
Ellipsis London Limited
SERIES EDITOR Tom Neville
SERIES DESIGN Jonathan Moberly
LAYOUT Pauline Harrison

COPYRIGHT © 1996 Könemann
Verlagsgesellschaft mbH
Bonner Str. 126, D-50968 Köln
PRODUCTION MANAGER Detlev Schaper
PRINTING AND BINDING Sing Cheong
Printing Ltd
Printed in Hong Kong

ISBN 3 89508 284 8 (Könemann)
ISBN 1 874056 81 1 (Ellipsis)

Susanna Sirefman 1994

Contents

Introduction

This book covers exactly 100 schemes, all designed and built within the last decade. While it is not meant to be a comprehensive guide, I hope the work I have chosen cumulatively represents the current trends of architecture in Chicago and is a diverse representation of both well-established firms and the new, fresh, up-and-coming design stars.

Beginning chronologically with 333 West Wacker Drive and The Associates Center, both significant projects from 1983 and ending with the Cesar Chavez Elementary School opened in autumn 1993, I have attempted to include a cross section of the diverse commercial, residential, industrial and public projects, both large and small, throughout the city and its suburbs. It is worth noting that the two earliest schemes are downtown office towers and the most recently completed project I have included is a public education facility in one of the less affluent areas of town. The crazy 1980s' boom of speculative commercial skyscrapers has definitely come to a screeching halt and is being replaced with an emphasis on civil work. It is very encouraging that the largest public project of the decade is the Harold Washington Library. Whether you care for the building or not, it is undeniably of huge social significance. Its location should go some way to reverse the dire recreational decline of the Loop area, where there is now a conspicuous shortage of restaurants, cinemas or entertainment activities, particularly at night-time.

The other recent federally funded building, the Thompson Center, is significant for the difference in its appearance, not so important for its aesthetic value but for the very fact that it was allowed to be built. It is depressing to witness the obvious difference in financial resources between a federal project such as the Thompson Center and the super lush, marble and granite extravaganzas along Wacker Drive. Contemporary and experimental architecture must be encouraged and supported and given the funding it deserves. Ideas must be given a chance. I believe the current somewhat reactionary vogue for historicism or contextual buildings must be tempered with a bit of daring and outrageousness. Fitting into the existing typology is of the utmost importance but has unfortunately been the cause of too many bland, nondescript structures. This is why it is so pleasing to happen upon projects such as Bertrand Goldberg's River City or Hartshorne Plunkard's Peter Elliott Productions Studios. Their very merit is in attempting something new and different, almost regardless of their success or failure.

North Michigan Avenue, one of America's poshest strip malls, also tells a fascinating story about the state of architecture (and economics) in the 1990s. The large and formidable complexes – 900 North Michigan Avenue, City Place and Chicago Place – are next door to the diminutive but fun Banana Republic, Crate & Barrel and the nondescript Escada Plaza. It would be refreshing but unrealistic to think that smaller, free-standing shops will replace the monstrous vertical malls being erected like mad just a couple of years ago.

The middle belt of residential properties ringing the downtown centre, most notable architecturally on the North Side of Chicago (Lincoln Park, Gold Coast and Old Town), is also of great interest as Chicagoans clearly have an affinity for living in houses. Most of the city is surprisingly flat, allowing for the family home to flourish along quiet residential streets. Accurately known as a city of neighbourhoods, sadly this clear division and delineation emphasises Chicago's extraordinary and unfortunate segregation. It was no surprise that there were no new architectural delights in the South Side residential areas. I hope the move towards less commercially motivated projects will spur some decent low-income public housing plans in the 1990s.

The decentralisation of downtown Chicago is in part a direct result of an enormous demographic shift over the last 20 odd years, the city oozing and seeping outwards and into the suburbs. For this reason I have included eighteen schemes located in the north and south Greater Chicago areas. As in most North American cities, the 'burbs are currently one of the most important growth and expansion areas of Chicago, as the trend of large corporations moving their offices out of downtown requires not only the creation of industrial parks (or the first skyscraper in Chicago's suburbia – Oakbrook Terrace Tower) but also infrastructure and housing for employees. Post-urban Chicago is continuously generating outwards, slowly urbanising an ever-increasing ring around its epicentre.

Aside from being America's best-known city of architecture, Chicago's spectacular geographical setting lends it a unique air of elegance. Considered world-wide the 'Home of the Skyscraper' (as a result of rebuilding after the Great Fire of 1871), the Chicago River and the lake surrounding the entire eastern half of the city (beaches and all!) creates a tranquil backdrop for this all-American city. The skyline is a spectacular mixture of industrial warehouses and factories, Beaux-Arts buildings, linear Mies juxtaposed with the many new and astounding forms the most contemporary buildings have taken on.

Standing on the top of the Sears Tower or the John Hancock Tower and surveying the rooftops is a wonderful way to enjoy the diversity of Chicago's buildings. The public transport system, in particular the 'L', is another good way to get an overview of Chicago. Snaking past many of the new buildings that I mention is as exciting as the boat ride down the river, another must do for all enthusiasts of contemporary architecture.

Acknowledgements

Thank you:
to all the architects I met with or spoke to for their time and the materials they so enthusiatically supplied; to all the photographers who so kindly contributed their work; to the Marketing Department at the Chicago Transit Authority for their advice on public transport; to my great friends in Chicago, Edward Moore and the Exley family; but most of all to Carol and Josef Sirefman for their tireless support, generosity and encouragement.
SS 1994

Using this book

The city has been divided into sixteen geographical sections, starting at the O'Hare International Airport and running roughly north to south before covering the suburbs. Bus and rapid transport train (RTT) routes from downtown are listed under each entry, and road directions for buildings outside the city's rapid transport system. I have given the station listing closest to each destination.

A useful number to have for emergency details is the CTA Travel Information Center. They will provide directions, schedules and fare information for the CTA bus, rapid transit system, Pace suburban buses and Metra trains. Open 05.00–01.00 daily, including holidays, their telephone number is 312 836 7000.

The CTA System Transit Map (constantly being updated) is available at the major transit stations, O'Hare Airport, all major hotels downtown and Visitor Information Centers. Passes and tokens are sold at banks and currency locations.

Chicago is also a wonderful city for walking, provided the weather is fair enough. If you are unfamiliar with the city do ask advice on where not to wander into, particularly on the South Side.

If you would like more architectural information, The Chicago Architecture Foundation (CAF), has a shop, gallery and tour center which offers over 50 walking, bicycle, boat and bus tours. They are located at 224 South Michigan Avenue at East Jackson Boulevard.

15, 16

1

2

3

4

5

7 6

9 8

10

11

12

13

14

1 O'Hare International Airport
2 Lakeview and Uptown Ravenswood
3 Lincoln Park
4 Gold Coast and Old Town
5 River North
6 Near North and Streeterville
7 North Michigan Avenue
8 East Loop
9 West Loop
10 Near West Side and South Loop
11 Pilsen
12 Near North Side and Bridgeport
13 Hyde Park
14 Suburbs South-West
15 Suburbs North
16 Gurnee and Zion

O'Hare International Airport

O'Hare International Airport opened in 1963 and is currently the nation's busiest with over 72 million passengers passing through in just one year. In 1982 Chicago's Department of Aviation initiated the $2 billion development plan due for completion in 1995. This master plan for rejuvenation and expansion was drawn up by a team composed of Murphy/Jahn, Environdyne Engineers, Inc., and Schal Associates. The strategy called for two new terminals, additional roadways, a new rapid transit station, services and a 240 acre cargo area. Murphy/Jahn, whose firm has had a historical link to the airport (throughout the airport's development the various stages of design and construction have been headed by the same architectural firm in its several incarnations: Naess & Murphy, C F Murphy & Associates and now Murphy/Jahn led by Helmut Jahn), designed the United Terminal and the peripheral transportation station linked to the new terminal.

Located on the same site as the former International Terminal, the new plan is designed to serve 70,000 travellers a day. Constrained by previously set rules – 747 wide-body jet size, taxiing patterns, site lines from the control tower and the already set length of the two pre-existing parallel concourses – Helmut Jahn has created a superb, calm, easy-to-negotiate terminal.

The structurally expressive terminal is entered under an industrial square-cornered stainless steel canopy that extends its entire length. Passengers leave the access roadway at the curb and enter a transitional vestibule leading to the light-filled Ticketing Pavilion. This grand open space was inspired by the magnificent waiting rooms of Victorian railroad sheds, exhibition halls and arcades with visible iron and glass skeletons. Treated as an island, the 1.2 million square foot terminal is focused around the two long, rectangular concourses, B and C, that run parallel

O'Hare International Airport

Murphy/Jahn 1982—1988

to the pavilion. The vast column-free Ticketing Pavilion is only an ante-room, albeit huge and capacious, leading to these terminal centres. The lower level below the ticketing area is the baggage claim. The free-span of 120 feet created by the folded truss system roof frame allows total flexibility for the 56 flow-through ticketing/baggage check counters in the pavilion. According to the architects 100 per cent of the lighting requirements during the day are met naturally. This is achieved by 5-foot-wide linear skylights placed at the peaks of the folded truss roof. Gull-wing baffles suspended underneath the skylights filter direct sunlight and house flourescent lamps and a relatively new type of low-wattage compact metal halide lamps for night illumination.

The monumental concourses are vaulted corridors constructed using a system of aluminium sandwich panels (which incorporate an acoustical inner surface) and glass units secured to the steel purlin substructure. The glazed units, varying between clear insulated, tinted insulated and clear-fritted glass, were arranged according to the most beneficial natural light and solar gain configurations. A ceramic frit pattern was fired directly to the inside surface of the inner lights in the system to allow transparency while reducing solar penetration and also effectively creating a reflective interior surface for indirect lighting at night. This innovative use of fritted glass in such quantity is a first in America.

The beautifully detailed structure of the vaults is accentuated by curved rolled steel beams placed at 30-foot intervals. Painted white and punched with circular holes to achieve lightness and transparency, the beams are supported by clusters of bundled columns (steel pipes in groups of one to five tubes depending on the load each column supports). These continue the length of each concourse, both of which terminate in semi-domed spaces. The effective sequence of spatial events culminates in the

Murphy/Jahn 1982—1988

concourse connection; the most wonderful 52-foot-wide and 815-foot-long pedestrian tunnel. Evocative of a New Age *Logan's Run* movie set, this novel corridor is entertaining and relaxing. The 800 foot, below-grade link, reached by an escalator, has a moving walkway surrounded by futuristic magical lighting, art and music. Undulating translucent glass walls and ceiling are backlit with a delightful range of colours. Stylistic steel 'trees' support the curvy, glowing membrane walls and ceiling plane. Above the four parallel moving sidewalks is a constantly changing light sculpture created by Michael Hayden. The neon light tubes hanging from a mirrored surface are controlled by a computer that generates patterns of light pulses that are never repeated. These changing colours, coordinated with the colours of the walls, are synchronised with atonal synthesised music composed by William Kraft and amended by Gary Fry. Great fun, this corridor brings a smile to even the most jaded passenger.

O'Hare International Airport

ASSOCIATE ARCHITECTS A Epstein & Sons
STRUCTURAL ENGINEERS Lev Zetlin Associates and A Epstein & Sons
RTT Blue Line
ACCESS public areas open

Murphy/Jahn 1982—1988

O'Hare International Airport

Murphy/Jahn 1982—1988

O'Hare Rapid Transit Station

Very much a gateway, this station is the primary public transport link between downtown Chicago and O'Hare Airport.

Allowing two column-free platforms, a system of large post-tensioned concrete girders constructed around the parking garage columns are set in an open-cut excavation. This configuration resulted in sloping berms running the length of the station. These earth mounds were concrete sprayed and concealed behind undulating glass block walls. Ribbed glass blocks alternate with translucent bricks behind which the berm has been painted in a progression of colours. The changing pattern of blocks, from transparency to opacity and back, is reinforced by the intensity of pastel colour. The combination of the 30-foot curving wall, gradated, incandescent colour and backlit glass blocks creates a warm, kinetic ambience. The rippling walls also reduce the noise level from the trains. The vocabulary of materials throughout the station – stainless steel benches, handrails, platform carrels and the black rubberised flooring – revolve around the underground train theme and heavy usage requirements.

The long, curving concourse has been treated as a transitional space and is in muted tones of grey, black and white. Horizontal bands of glazed brick reverse in colour at the terminal entrances and symbolic gateways are marked by bright red columns supporting a tiled glazed brick entablature that are derivative of classical patterns.

ASSOCIATE ARCHITECT Murphy/Jahn
STRUCTURAL ENGINEERS Alfred Benesch & Co.
SIZE 105,000 square feet (9750 square metres)
CLIENT City of Chicago, Department of Public Works
RTT Blue Line
ACCESS public

City of Chicago, Dept of Public Works, Bureau of Architecture 1984

O'Hare International Airport

City of Chicago, Dept of Public Works, Bureau of Architecture 1984

International Terminal

The final large piece of the $2 billion O'Hare redevelopment scheme, the International Terminal accommodates foreign-flag departures and all international arrivals. It houses a ticketing pavilion, twenty-one gates, concessions, support facilities, a transit station and Federal Inspection Services. The terminal is organised around three primary levels: the upper contains the departure hall, the lower level is the 'meeters and greeters' area and the middle, intermediate level is for baggage processing. Administration occupies a fourth mezzanine level. The 100-acre triangular site determined the boundaries of the design as it is bordered by taxiways, runways, and the entrance roadway. Set at some distance from the other terminals and parking facilities at O'Hare, there is a delightful above-ground light rail transit system that follows a dramatic curvy track and provides a spectacular approach to the new terminal.

A soaring vertical arch, the terminal is beautiful and streamlined. As at the United Terminal, the inspiration was early 19th-century railway stations although here it has been given a completely different twist. An 800-foot-long ticketing pavilion has a gently arched roof that curves up from 14 to 50 feet. The departure hall benefits the most from the exposed structural steel system, enclosed by expansive glazed sidewalls. From this hall, passengers enter the galleria which is directly under the curving roof, functioning as a guide towards the airline departure gates.

The major materials – glass curtain wall and skylights, fluted metal and metal panel siding, painted concrete block, plastic laminate and precast terrazo tile – all speak an industrial language appropriate and familiar from airport structures such as hangars and warehouses.

Security has put a fair amount of restraint on circulation within the terminal and unfortunately movement through the building is not as streamlined as the overall structure. Surprisingly small, the dimensions

Perkins & Will 1993

Perkins & Will 1993

of such a new and ambitious facility seem extremely restricted and there is talk of further expansion. Perhaps more energy should have gone into the initial masterplanning phase to produce an overall scheme capable of properly accommodating future growth.

ASSOCIATE ARCHITECTS Heard & Associates, Consoer Townsend & Associates
STRUCTURAL ENGINEERS Wells Engineering
CLIENT City of Chicago Department of Aviation
COST $618 million
SIZE 1,145,000 square feet (106,000 square metres)
RTT Blue Line
ACCESS to public areas

O'Hare International Airport

Perkins & Will 1993

O'Hare International Airport

Perkins & Will 1993

Lakeview and Uptown Ravenswood

Chicago City Day School Addition

This very smart addition to a private elementary school houses a gym, auditorium, labs and a dining room. Set against the back of the triangular site, this stylish extension blends well into its posh residential surroundings. The existing three-storey classroom building dates from the 1960s.

The new exterior is of limestone, in stark contrast to the old building's dark brick. The architects were clearly inspired by Eero and Eliel Saarinenn's Crow Island School. An assymetric clock tower sheathed in stainless steel adds a vertical element to the façade. Windows at a child's scale and a low protective entrance canopy rhythmically energise the limestone façade.

Lakeview and Uptown Ravenswood

ADDRESS 541 West Hawthorne Place
STRUCTURAL ENGINEERS Robert L Miller Associates
COST $2.64 million
SIZE 22,800 square feet (2100 square metres)
RTT Belmont on Red Line, Brown Line, Purple Line Express
BUS 8, 36, 77, 135, 145, 146, 152, 156
ACCESS none

Weese Langley Weese 1990

Weese Langley Weese 1990

Chicago Public Library, Conrad Sulzer Regional Branch

The firm of Hammond, Beeby and Babka has quite a track record in building libraries, having designed them throughout suburban Illinois in Champaign, Skokie, Tinley Park, Northbrook and Oak Park as well as for the Kansas State University in Manhattan, Kansas. Best-known is the Harold Washington Library, smack in the middle of the Loop.

One of the highest circulation branches in Chicago's regional library system, the Conrad Sulzer holds 250,000 books. The design was five years off the drawing board before it was actually constructed because of bureaucratic red tape.

The triangular site, bounded by the diagonally bisecting Lincoln Avenue and east–west Sunnyside Avenue, is directly opposite a city park. The building is intended to be a link between commercial Lincoln Avenue and the ethnically rich residential surrounding neighbourhood. Treated as an object, the building is a long rectangle with a semicircular front. The façade on Lincoln Avenue comes to the pavement edge and continues the height level of the existing stores and shops. The back of the building, which contains the non-public services, has less assertive massing.

Head designer Thomas Beeby describes the library as 'hybrid Mies and Schinckel'. The nod to German neo-Classicism was an acknowledgement of the ethnic flavour of Ravenswood. The heavy façade is evocative of traditional civic institutions. The thick brick walls give the impression of substance as well as housing mechanical systems. There is very little interior visibility from the street and, for security reasons, the steel-outlined setback windows are barred and locked.

The interior is filled with natural light and is as friendly as the exterior is imposing. The entrance lobby, a beautiful elliptical rotunda two storeys

Hammond, Beeby & Babka

Lakeview and Uptown Ravenswood

Joseph Casserly/Chicago City Architect 1985

above a terrazzo floor, provides access to the auditorium and a public meeting room. These spaces can be used when the rest of the library is shut, creating an important neighbourhood gathering place.

As you walk up the stairs to the second level there is a marvellously powerful view of eight 20-foot columns parading down the centre of the room. These fabulous giant black pillars are also exposed function – they are the air-circulation system. A large fun clock hangs in the middle of the space over a circular computer station.

Another enjoyable element of this public facility is the furniture. Architect Tannys Langdon has created charming folk chairs that celebrate the Teutonic theme. Dotted throughout the library, they tell mythical tales based on German fables and mythology. In the children's section, child-sized chairs and a special combination chair-table are constructed of plywood and surface paint.

The local community was closely involved in the development and decoration of the library. In fact, a fresco by Irene Siegal entitled 'Aenead' had to be removed from the meeting room as the text the artist had painted into the mural was interpreted by the neighbourhood as graffiti. There was general outrage that public money was paying for what the neighbourhood perceived as illegal and disrespectful!

ADDRESS 4455 North Lincoln Avenue
CLIENT Conrad Sulzer Regional Library
COST $7.6 million
SIZE 62,700 square feet (5800 square metres)
RTT Western on Brown Line
BUS 11, 49, 49B, 78
ACCESS public

Hammond, Beeby & Babka

Lakeview and Uptown Ravenswood

Joseph Casserly/Chicago City Architect 1985

Lincoln Park

BMT Offices

This uppermost floor of a 1910 industrial warehouse has been renovated for a small toy-design company. Fragmented drywall planes, unexpected angles and colourful cubic partitions in primary colours – red, blue and yellow – create a complex anti-orthogonal plan. A yellow wedge is visible on the exterior rear façade bursting out of the thick red brick wall signalling the office's existence to the passing world.

Security and the fear of industrial espionage caused the public areas and the design laboratory space to be separated. Included in the programme is a toy demonstration stage for the unveiling of new playthings. After journeying through a succession of doors in the common rooms there is an open-plan design studio with the confidential toy-making workshop. The whole loft is then connected by an overhead miniature train keeping to the toy theme permeating the 30-person office.

ADDRESS 750 North Orleans
CLIENT Rouben Terzian and BMT Design
SIZE 4800 square feet (445 square metres)
RTT Chicago on Brown Line, Purple Line Express
BUS 37, 41, 66
ACCESS none

Lincoln Park

Pappageorge Haymes 1988

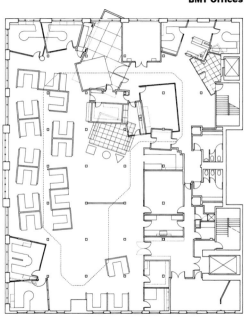

Pappageorge Haymes 1988

Florian Twoflat

The striking cream and grey street elevation of this two-storey wooden-frame house is descriptive of the building's structural history and reflects the designers' preoccupations. A juxtaposition of two urban building types, attention is called to the twenty odd years between the construction of the top and bottom of the house. The downstairs is a straightforward post-and-beam rowhouse while the top, added on later, is a typical balloon-frame Chicago bungalow.

The lower half of the façade has three perfectly proportioned window columns placed within a raised rectilinear grid. This topographical geometry is repeated in the horizontal ornament of the front garden enclosure. Representative of urban order, these silhouettes of classical configuration are playful gestures suggesting formality. The simple top half, a vernacular bungalow perched on the stripped classical base, is punctuated by irregular fenestration. One square window is unexpectedly placed directly on top of the cornice line and the other is just a narrow hint of an opening. In the centre is a vertical pillar of windows and a miniature balcony with a charming linear balustrade that links the two halves.

The upper apartment's interior, reached by a staircase to the second floor, is a colourful combination of Russian Constructivist, Deconstructivist and De Stijl influences. Various planes have been pulled, shifted and reoriented, giving this small 750-square-foot studio apartment an open and spacious air.

The layout is one long rectangle centred around a free-standing cube. A skewed red triangular slab slices through the top of the white floating kitchen wall, and connects all the elements of the space. Extending diagonally through the apartment, this level plane, which is the structural support for the sleeping loft, juts into the shower room and transforms into the kitchen ceiling. This element connects all the functionally sepa-

Florian-Wierzbowski 1986

Florian-Wierzbowski 1986

rate areas of the apartment.

An arcade of repeating green doors lengthens the perspective of the white entry wall. Windows have been placed quite high for privacy as the lot is enclosed by buildings on either side. There is a wonderfully subtle match between the green wall and the next-door roof slats that is visible out of these raised windows, and changes with the daily travel of the sun. All the carefully chosen colours throughout the project – greens, brilliant yellow, an orange pink and blue – highlight specific forms and therefore call attention to their interaction. An example of this is the yellow kitchen shelf that penetrates into the living room, creating a fabulous composition of linear colour and form.

A condition that is repeated at all scales, the floor of the apartment extends as a deck, hanging over the backyard, and is treated as a breakfast nook. This cantilevered treehouse deck is shaded by a pear-tree. Form, function and process have clearly been intellectually explored and most delightfully expressed.

Lincoln Park

ADDRESS 1816 North Cleveland Street
CLIENT Paul Florian
SIZE 750 square feet (70 square metres)
RTT Sedgwick on Brown Line (B stop)
BUS 11, 37, 72, 73
ACCESS none

Florian-Wierzbowski 1986

Florian-Wierzbowski 1986

Mohawk Street House

Rigorous symmetry, inside and out, characterises this contemporary three-storey city house. Adjacent to an empty lot and surrounded by older weathered threeflats, this private home is located in a slightly rundown residential neighbourhood. The simple vertically oriented exterior of brick and concrete has an unexpected cupola on top. The apparently narrow façade, with a recessed entranceway, actually hides a surprisingly spacious interior. This illusion is intentional and Frederick Phillips plays with this theme throughout the project.

Each floor is 900 square feet, a studio flat occupying most of the first floor. The remaining two levels are each divided into three. The second floor revolves around a central dining space, separated from the kitchen and living room by frames with doors that can slide out if desired. The lack of solid enclosure between areas produces a feeling of space and openness. A skylight at the top centre of the house not only lets sunlight in (there are no side windows) but becomes an organising element for the three bedrooms on the upper storey. Curved walls caused by the insertion of a spiral staircase leading to the cupola add character to these bedrooms.

The interior is finished in subtle shades of white and cream. Natural light makes lovely shadows throughout. Everything seems to be perfectly placed, fitting together just so, like a super-neat sock drawer.

ADDRESS 1518 North Mohawk Street
STRUCTURAL ENGINEERS Beer Gorski & Graff
CLIENT Frederick and Gay Phillips
SIZE 2700 square feet (250 square metres)
RTT Sedgwick on Brown Line (B stop)
BUS 37, 72
ACCESS none

Lincoln Park

Frederick F Phillips & Associates 1989

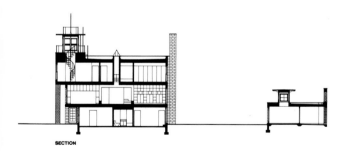

1

SECTION

Frederick F Phillips & Associates 1989

Scoozi!

Jordan Mozer and Rich Melman, president of Lettuce Entertain You Enterprises, have transformed a former auto-repair garage into a spacious warehouse restaurant, easily identifiable by the huge 652 pound fibreglass tomato hanging on the façade. A pleasantly crowded dark wood bar is theatrically set against the front wall as the focal point of the three-tiered 320-seat dining area. There are excellent people-watching views from most vantage points. The bright and cheery kitchen is at the back of the large, open space. The ambience is very New York vogue.

Distressed walls, mosaic floor, Renaissance-style moulding combined with antique fixtures lend a fashionable pseudo-historical feel. The discoloured, cracking walls look as though they have met with a great deal of aggression. The tormented result was achieved by overplastering, overheating, and then smashing at the plaster with sledge hammers.

Mozer kept the existing ceiling trusses, allowing the 100-foot clear span, and used these wooden planks to hang industrial chandeliers, an odd addition, particularily the rectangular Art Deco fixtures, as they diminish the well-worn, traditional image, as do the Italian magazines haphazardly wallpapered onto the low space dividers.

ADDRESS 410 West Huron Street
CLIENT Lettuce Entertain You Enterprises, Inc.
COLLABORATORS Aumiller Youngquist p.c.
COST $1.9 million
SIZE 13,000 square feet (1200 square metres)
RTT Chicago/Franklin on Brown Line, Purple Line
BUS 37, 41, 66
ACCESS lunch Monday through Friday and dinner seven nights

Lincoln Park

Jordan Mozer & Associates, Limited 1987

Jordan Mozer & Associates, Limited 1987

Cairo

Another trendy Mozer-designed nightspot, the theme for this jazz club is Egypt. Legend has it that Mozer was struck by the loaded symbolism and fantasy of the client's girlfriend's goldleaf earrings. Mozer then spent over a year steeped in Egyptology. From the naming of this two-level establishment through to the downstairs dance floor with private catacombs, the sarcophagus-like entry and the generous distribution of lapis lazuli inlay, the Egyptian notion has inspired the plan, materials and details. Lacquered wood, oxidised copper and the expected decaying walls add that archaeological touch. Even the maple zigzag bar takes the form of the hieroglyph for water.

As in all his imaginative and inventive spaces, Mozer adds novel contemporary touches. At Cairo the piano is hiding in a wonderful curving free-standing partition and the light fixtures are Art Deco. The furniture – in particular the Cairo chair, a pudgy upholstered seat on a steel frame held together by automotive lug nuts – is quite charming. This chair is now being manufactured in a limited edition by Shelby Williams.

In admirable merchandising style Mozer has expanded into home furnishings; the furniture at other Mozer-designed venues (Sabrina, Neo, Scoozi! and Vivere) besides Cairo is now being made to order.

ADDRESS 720 North Wells Street (at West Superior Street)
CLIENT John Abell
COST $840,000
SIZE 5500 square feet (510 square metres)
RTT Chicago/Franklin on Brown Line, Purple Line Express
BUS 11, 22, 36, 37, 41, 135, 136, 156
ACCESS Tuesday–Friday 20.00–04.00; Saturdayand Sunday 21.00–04.00

Lincoln Park

Jordan Mozer & Associates 1988

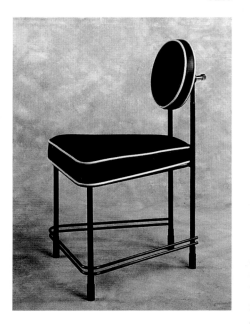

Jordan Mozer & Associates 1988

Luminaire

This converted loft shop is designer furniture heaven. An industrial steel bridge leads through a floating glass entranceway into a quiet interior that shows off the beautiful chairs, beds, lighting fixtures and art/architecture books at their best, allowing them to be splashes of colour against the store's predominantly neutral palette. Sandblasted glass partitions hover over the white wood floor in between stretches of exposed brick wall creating little niches for the various categories of display in this studiously chic ambience. A serious, trendy place in which many young architects spend their lunch hours dreaming of owning all these gorgeous designer wares.

ADDRESS 301 West Superior
CLIENT Nasir-Kassamau Luminaire
COST $247,000
SIZE 12,455 square feet (1160 square metres)
RTT Chicago/Franklin on Brown Line, Purple Line Express
BUS 37, 41, 66
ACCESS open during normal shopping hours

Lincoln Park

Pappageorge Haymes 1992

Pappageorge Haymes 1992

Embassy Club

The Embassy Club is the latest of Pappageorge Haymes' monopoly of Lincoln Park housing developments. City Commons (intersection of Willow, Orchard & Vine) was the first complex completed in 1985, and Larrabee Commons (intersection of North Avenue, Larrabee and Mohawk), Altgeld Court (1300 West Altgeld) and the Clybourn Lofts (1872 North Clybourn) followed.

The Embassy Club luxury homes are a witty, solidly built play on the English townhouse. Lined up in straight (or the odd curving formation) terraced rows, the ornamentation on the façade and size of the bay windows seems to reveal the house's cost, setting up a rather feudal little enclave.

ADDRESS intersection of Wrightwood,
Greenview, Southport
CLIENT MCL Construction Corporation
STRUCTURAL ENGINEERS Samartano & Co.,
Abatangelo & Hason
COST $15 million
SIZE 412,262 square feet
(38,300 square metres)
RTT Fullerton on Brown Line, Red Line,
Purple Line Express
BUS 9, 74, 76
ACCESS none

Lincoln Park

Pappageorge Haymes 1993

Pappageorge Haymes 1993

Lincoln Park

Gold Coast and Old Town

House of Light

Nicknamed by the architects Casa della Luce, not only because of the extraordinary amount of natural light pouring in through skylights and huge windows but also because of the playfulness of the designed lighting fixtures floating throughout the house. At night the house has the capacity to be flooded with as many subtleties of light as during daylight hours. Delicate, elegant and radiant, everything about this house glows.

A green wrought-iron fence is the first announcement connected to the cool façade (limestone veneer over masonry) that supports a glazed vestibule (the only questionable space, this lobby is extremely formal, a bit too impersonal in comparison to the warmth of the rest of the house).

The house is organised symmetrically around a central three-storey skylight core with stairways wrapping round a rectangular opening. The dining room surrounded by columns and architraves is at the bottom of the atrium, set a few inches above the living room. These split-level floors elongate the plan, opening up the already voluminous-feeling space. The second floor has the master bedroom and a formal library/study with a giant oculus that is part of the intricate lighting plan, creating internal sunshine. The third floor, continuing the theme of understated colour modulations for each space (adding another lovely dimension to the play of light), has a children's bedroom with a comforting low ceiling and an informal guest bedroom.

ADDRESS 1828 North Orleans Street
STRUCTURAL ENGINEERS Chris P Stefanos Associates
SIZE 5124 square feet (476 square metres)
RTT Sedgwick on Brown Line (B stop)
BUS 11, 22, 36, 37, 73
ACCESS none

Booth Hansen & Associates 1983

Booth Hansen & Associates 1983

Chicago Historical Society Addition

Founded in 1857, in 1931 the Chicago Historical Society moved into a 105,219 square foot Georgian Revival building designed by Graham, Anderson, Probst & White. This grand redbrick and limestone building sits on the south-west corner of Lincoln Park. In 1971 a 53,875 square foot annex was built, designed by Alfred Shaw & Associates. The main access was shifted to Clark Street, but the white marble entrance created an intimidating image. The latest addition has a welcoming street façade and neutralises the stylistic differences of the old and new. Gerald Horn led the Holabird & Root team in establishing a new identity for the building and improving its programmatic functions.

The 1988 addition conceals the 1971 edifice, wrapping the west elevation in a skin of red brick, Indiana limestone, glass and steel. These materials, and the scale of the new structure, although stylistically unassociated, meld well with the original. As the museum is situated on city park land the available new space was quite restricted, with any addition pretty well contained within the existing building's perimeters. This required extensive structural modifications, and cladding from the building was removed to reduce the load on structural members. The second floor, originally 23 feet high, was divided into two floors, doubling the gallery space within the same enclosure.

The public entrance, of glass curtain wall grid and white steel trusses, has a pointed steel pediment from which bright banners announcing the exhibits are hung. Grids are everywhere. The black, rust and white gridded marble lobby floor is enclosed by a wonderful grid wall installation on either side of the main staircase (which has a gridded railing), and a gridded viewing bridge over the entranceway. Twenty square niches forming a grid parade some of the Society's 20 million artefacts. These are all objects used or made in Chicago. Life-size exhibits about Illinois

Holabird & Root 1988

Holabird & Root 1988

pioneer life and frontier Chicago continue in the galleries. There are rooms full of dioramas depicting Chicago's swift growth in the nineteenth century, an hands on interactive gallery, and a time capsule sitting in the lobby waiting to be unsealed in 2038.

A public restaurant, staff lounge and the Historical Society gift shop are housed in the three-storey curving glass wall facing south towards North Avenue.

ADDRESS 1601 Clark Street (at West North Avenue)
CLIENT Chicago Historical Society
SIZE 93,820 square feet (8700 square metres)
COST $11 million
RTT North/Sedgwick on Brown Line B, Clark/Division on Red Line
BUS 11, 22, 36, 72, 135, 136, 151, 156
ACCESS Monday–Saturday 09.30–16.30; Sunday 12.00–17.00 (entrance free on Monday). Closed for Thanksgiving, Christmas Day and New Year's Day

Holabird & Root 1988

Holabird & Root 1988

Victorian Townhouse Extended

The wide alleyways between streets are an intrinsic part of Chicago's plan. Usually simply passageways to garages, back gardens, or depositories for rubbish, the alleyway between Dearborn and Clark Streets has a remarkable architectural surprise. An extension of a demure Victorian townhouse juts out in colourful glory. One of the few examples of Deconstructivism in Chicago, this addition is a wild paroxysm of clashing angles, planes, colours and forms. Starting with hints of fragmentation in the interior, the house explodes into the alleyway in a flash of blue, gold and pink glass, battered/warped aluminium and mirrored curling stairways. A spectacular, dizzying sight!

ADDRESS 1522 North Dearborn
STRUCTURAL ENGINEERS Gullaksen, Getty & White
SIZE 5000 square feet (465 square metres)
RTT edgwick on Brown Line B, Clark/Division on Red Line
BUS 11, 22, 36, 37, 72, 135, 136, 151, 156
ACCESS none

Krueck and Olsen 1985

Krueck and Olsen 1985

Playboy Enterprises Corporate Headquarters

The first thing you see as you step out of the lift at Playboy's elegant and modern penthouse offices is a giant bronze Rabbit Head sculpture, Richard Hunt's interpretation of the famous logo. The groovy energetic 30-foot-high lobby is anchored by a freeform reception desk, a lunar pearl Black Andes granite and sand-blasted elliptical top supported by wavy poured concrete wiggles. The exterior of the elevator bank clad in an exotic, warm, African wood, avodire, that resembles washed silk, offsets the cold terrazzo floors inlaid with stainless steel lines.

The central atrium, a long galley designed to be the central circulation spine as well as an art gallery for Playboy's art collection, is carpeted in a sumptuously camp purple. A 160-foot-long skylight from the second storey sends sunlight bouncing off bowed stainless steel canopies and aeronauticalish curved steel soffits into the back office spaces. A huge Tom Wesselman painting of crimson smiling lips waits at the top of one of the terrazzo staircases. Perforated metal fins pivot to display more art and to separate work areas from common ground. Most of the office space is open plan, but the executive offices have translucent panels separating them from the long, rectangular atrium.

ADDRESS 680 North Lake Shore Drive
STRUCTURAL ENGINEERS Kolbjorn Saether & Associates
SIZE 100,000 square feet (9300 square metres)
CLIENT Playboy Enterprises, Inc.
RTT Grand/State or Chicago/State on Red Line
BUS 3, 29, 56, 65, 66, 120, 121, 157
ACCESS none

Gold Coast and Old Town

Himmel Bonner Architects 1989

Himmel Bonner Architects 1989

Steel & Glass House

Mies van der Rohe's rectangular glass and steel house was a starting point for Krueck and Olsen's first project together. Both trained in Chicago (ITT). They have reverently incorporated many Mies ideals, adding their own special twist.

A two-storey steel-frame structure (a prefabricated steel angle framing system) forming a U-shaped plan, the house is 5000 square feet located on a 67 x 127 foot corner plot. The flat plane of the steel lattice is accentuated by the narrow red metal stripe following the grid line. To create an ambience of privacy the centre of the house (with access to the rest of the building) is reached by passing through a series of parallel layers. The circular drive, partially hidden behind an iron spot brick wall, leads up to the industrial–style façade. A screen of subway grating camouflages the back of the cylindrical glass block stair tower. This façade is illuminated by a continuous neon billboard tube at night to spectacular effect. The entrance is on the west side of the horseshoe and off the terrazzo-floored foyer is a cloakroom and the garage with the master bedroom suite above on the second level and a stairway off the first level leading to the basement gym. The focal point of the U is the 70 x 22 foot living room.

Materials differentiate the four exterior sides of the house, the front and rear elevations are glass and the sides are metal allowing privacy from the dense residential neighbourhood. The front south-facing wall of the living room is floor-to-ceiling glass looking out on the small courtyard and allowing natural light to fall on the wonderful Richard Long wall painting covering the entire rear wall. The entire house is currently filled with contemporary art, including Claes Oldenburg sculpture and Barbara Kruger collages.

A housekeeper's quarters, kitchen and dining room occupy the eastern

Krueck & Olsen 1985

Krueck & Olsen 1985

section of the U on the ground floor with a guest bedroom, bathroom, and study above. The study masks a wet bar behind it, useful for entertaining. A skylit steel and glass-block walkway hangs over the living room connecting the two wings.

Interior surfaces are softer and more luxurious than the cold façade. Greys, maroons and dark greens are explored in marbles, velvets and lacquered woods. This steel and glass house is an elegantly precise and voluptuous container, a satisfying modern balance of urbanity and homeliness.

ADDRESS 1949 North Larrabee
STRUCTURAL ENGINEERS Gullaksen & Getty
SIZE 3000 square feet (280 square metres)
RTT Armitage on Brown Line
BUS 8, 11, 37, 73
ACCESS none

Krueck & Olsen 1985

Krueck & Olsen 1985

House with a Bay

Squeezed into a 24-foot-wide lot, this small townhouse's most remarkable feature is the large bay on the front façade. The building is a tribute to the art of ornamentation and the Chicago School.

The structure is masonry, using 'Chicago Common', hard-faced red brick on the elevations. The front façade functions as a modest background for the marvellous geometric bay stuck smack in the centre. The framework is constructed of moulded fibreglass that resembles metal. Curved and straight glass sections are set into it. The ornament is based on a Victorian composition of circles in a square, used by Sullivan in his early work, and common to the Lincoln Park neighbourhood. The smooth red brick is also a familiar sight. The embellishment is repeated in three different sizes, on the red terracotta mouldings, the cornice and the plain terracotta sills. Similiar decorative circles appear in the iron picket fence. This motif persists throughout the interior. The fireplace and the kitchen have ornamental tiles made from the same moulds and even the layout of the internal spaces has been loosely based on this theme.

The ground floor has a guestroom at the front and a children's playroom at the back, opening onto the garden. The bay allows natural light into the living room, and together with the ten-foot high ceiling creates an airy, open, ambience.

ADDRESS 1873 North Orchard Street
STRUCTURAL ENGINEERS Beer Gorski & Graff
SIZE 3200 square feet (300 square metres)
RTT Armitage on Brown Line
BUS 8, 73
ACCESS none

Nagle, Hartray & Associates 1986

Nagle, Hartray & Associates 1986

Schiller Street Town Houses

Nagle, Hartray & Associates received the commission for this project after the client saw a house they had designed in Lincoln Park in 1985. This house (1852 North Orchard Street) became the prototype for the Schiller Street development. Oriented towards the quiet, residential Schiller Street, the brick townhouses are located on the corner of busy LaSalle Street. An exercise exhibiting the lyrical potential of repetition, all five of the townhouses have an identical front elevation and plan.

The garage and main entry face north, allowing the back garden to face south. A rhythmic series of two-storey bays protrude symmetrically from the flat grey brick veneer façade, overhanging the driveway. These cylinders contain two sets of curved gridded glass windows set in limestone sills. This manipulation of bold forms is similar to local 1930s' residences in the Chicago Modern style. Glass block detailing, metal piperail fences and metal entry gates add a layer of detail. The first level is organised around the service space, garage, entry and garden room. Living, dining and kitchen areas are on the second storey. On the second level there is an internal double-height skylight central court, allowing natural light in. Bedrooms are on the top floor, organised around the skylit space and linked by a bridge.

ADDRESS 141–149 West Schiller Street
STRUCTURAL ENGINEERS Beer Gorski & Graff
COST $1.66 million
SIZE 3500 square feet (325 square metres) each
RTT Clark/Division on Red Line, Sedgwick on Brown Line (B stop)
BUS 11, 22, 36, 135, 136, 145, 146, 147, 156
ACCESS none

Gold Coast and Old Town

Nagle, Hartray & Associates 1988

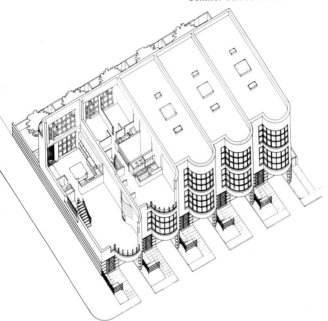

Nagle, Hartray & Associates 1988

River North

Hard Rock Café

A giant electric guitar rotates on the corner of the Hard Rock parking lot – you are now in Tacky Theme Park, Chicago. To be fair, the Hard Rock was built about eight years before the official River North Corridor Gimmick Invasion. Now its pseudo-orangerie façade seems positively serious. Designed to relate contextually to the original neo-Georgian Commonwealth Edison Substation next door, the Café has Tuscan proportions and neo-Palladian fenestration. All the measurements for entablatures, pedestal, die, collonettes and the windows in the building were informed by the 1929 substation. Painted green trellises decorate the façades, reinforcing the 18th century grand conservatory imagery.

There are three recent buildings in the area, which is already home to the Rock'n'Roll McDonald's, Ed Debevic's and Oprah Winfrey's Eccentric restaurant amongst others, creating an enclave of Disney-inspired architecture. Directly adjacent to the Hard Rock is the most disturbing new building of all, Capone's Chicago, a one-room polychromatic box dedicated to immortalising the gangster. Façades are bright yellows and blues with framed portraits slapped on in the most tawdry fashion. The new, completely over-the-top, Planet Hollywood a bit further up the street sports plastic palms, pink and green canopies, roving spotlights and a gigantic, gaudy posterboard Godzilla.

ADDRESS 63 West Ontario Street at North Dearborn Street
SIZE 12,000 square feet (1100 square metres)
RTT Grand/State on Red Line
BUS 15, 22, 29, 36, 65, 135, 136, 156
ACCESS Monday–Thursday 11.00–24.00; Friday 11.00–01.00; Saturday 10.30–01.00; Sunday 11.00–23.00

River North

Tigerman Fugman McCurry 1985

Tigerman Fugman McCurry 1985

Commonwealth Edison Substation

A few years after the Hard Rock Café was designed to complement the old substation, roles were reversed and the new substation (replacing the original) now takes its design cues from the Hard Rock. This duplicate reciprocity has resulted in two adjacent buildings with a similiar frame of reference and a close contextual relationship.

The new building incorporates actual fragments of the old as well as being stylistically similiar. Medallions and a plaque from the original façade, along with portions of the wrought-iron fence, are prominently displayed in Tigerman's scheme. The Indiana limestone elements, pilasters and entablatures are constructed through the wall, not just stuck on.

The only clue that this building's function is as an industrial utility is that large mechanical vents instead of glass fill the limestone window surrounds.

Part of the brief was that the building should be maintenance free. Therefore the architects chose to use dense and dimensionally stable FBX brick laid in English cross-bond.

ADDRESS 600 North Dearborn Street at West Ontario
STRUCTURAL ENGINEERS Beer Gorski & Graff
CLIENT Commonwealth Edison
SIZE 33,297 square feet (3100 square metres)
RTT Grand/State on Red Line
BUS 15, 22, 29, 36, 65, 135, 136, 156
ACCESS none

River North

Tigerman McCurry 1989

Tigerman McCurry 1989

American Medical Association Headquarters

Impressive use of negative space is evident in this Modernist building. A square, four-storey chunk of skyscraper has been cut out near the apex of this thirty-storey trapezoidal tower. Evocative as a refined, practical version of Gordon Matta-Clark's famous work – in particular 'Day's End' and 'Conical Intersect' (both 1975) in which Matta-Clark sliced large-scale geometrical sections from existing buildings – the hole in the American Medical Association Headquarters was designed to make the building an easily identifiable landmark. Such powerful spatial manipulation not only makes the project unique, it becomes exciting and thought-provoking. Removing a cube from an off-centre section of the upper middle of the building creates an ambiguity of scale. It is a powerful architectural gesture that forces the viewer to recognise the structure as a volumetric form in its own right.

The AMA owns eight blocks, roughly 12 acres in the River North region. The headquarters building is phase one of an ambitious urban redevelopment scheme. Kenzo Tange Associates (who title themselves Urbanists-Architects) were commissioned to draw up a masterplan for the entire site. This is Tange's first large commercial venture in the USA.

The new edifice is the first of a future pair. Both have been designed as trapezoids to 'maximise the sense of space and minimise the visual exposure to each other', according to the firm's publicity.

Structurally, the foundation is steel frame and the tower itself is steel frame with reinforced concrete. A glass and aluminium curtain wall rises elegantly from the flecked granite base. The exterior landscaping echoes the sharp, angular shape of the building. The dignified lobby has bonsai plants and a wonderful clear crackle-glass partition separating the

Kenzo Tange Associates 1990

River North

elevator banks.

Part of the project brief was to provide public exhibition space. The ama accommodates one of the three galleries of The Chicago Athenaeum, an independent international museum of architecture. Founded in 1988, the proclaimed aim of the foundation is to educate the public about good design. They could not have chosen a more apt location.

ADDRESS 515 North State Street and Grand Avenue
CO-ORDINATING ARCHITECTS Shaw & Associates, Inc.
STRUCTURAL ENGINEERS Cohen Barreto Marchertas, Inc.
CLIENT American Medical Association in a joint venture with developers Buck Company and Miller-Klutznick-Davis-Gray and Company
RTT Grand on Red Line
BUS 15, 29, 36, 65
ACCESS public lobby and gallery

River North

Kenzo Tange Associates 1990

Kenzo Tange Associates 1990

River Cottages

With a working drawbridge to one side and elevated train tracks to the rear, these posh townhouses are situated in one of the most interesting, atmospheric locations in Chicago. This piece of prominent riverfront, across from Wolf Point, was the site of Chicago's first railroad depot. Completed in 1848, it was the final destination of the Galena and Chicago Union Railroad. Freight trains would transport grain from all over the Midwest to this spot where the cargo was loaded onto schooners and shipped down the river. Disused railroad tracks are still charmingly visible, half buried among pathways and the greenery around the site. Adding to the mood, boats float past under the lifted authentic Kinzie Avenue drawbridge.

River Cottages is a project of personal interest to the architect, Harry Weese, who originally intended to live in one of the townhouses. The scheme allowed Weese to explore nautical themes and their architectural interpretations, a long-time interest.

Built symmetrically around an existing tree, River Cottages consists of four luxury townhouses in two attached buildings. Two of these four family homes have 4400 square feet of space on six levels and two have 2200 square feet of space on five levels. The long, narrow floors of all four are connected by stairs as well as individual elevators. The ground-floor entry is on North Canal Street but all the homes are oriented toward the river. From the inside, the views out at the Chicago skyline are spectacular. The interiors of the units were kept unfinished so that the buyers could do as they liked. This was not as great a success as expected, although the units went very quickly. Apparently the buyers would have preferred finished interiors. The suggested layout which most of the units follow is the living room, dining room and kitchen on the first floor, the master bedroom on the second, with additional bedrooms on the third, a study on the fourth

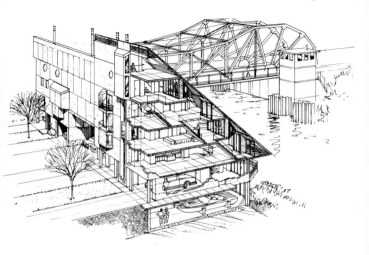

Harry Weese & Associates 1990

and a roof deck on the fifth.

All of the steeply sloping units have triangular balconies, spiral staircases, green metal decks, skylights and angled windows. These were inspired by schooner sails, boat riggings and lookout posts. The lovely curlicued stairs, juxtaposed with the severe angles of the sloped roof, present a fascinating, avant-garde façade. This complicated building suits its ideal site well. Surrounded by poplars, silver maples and flowering crab trees, it is a perfect retreat.

The exterior of the first three storeys is rubberised stucco. The geometrical upper half of the structure is steel and glass. The entire structure is cantilevered off the back concrete wall. Exposed tubular steel crossbracing is evident on the top floors of the two shorter homes. These mechanics have allowed the river façade of the building to have large triangular windows and peaked roofs.

This recently rejuvenated area has another Harry Weese & Associates' project (completed in 1981) a bit further down the river at number 345 North Canal Street. The Fulton House Condominium building is a converted warehouse. Built originally for the North American Cold Storage Company, the thickly insulated walls now house residential units.

ADDRESS 357–365 North Canal Street
STRUCTURAL ENGINEERS Harry Weese and Seymour Lepp & Associates
CLIENT Harry Weese
COST $2.5 million
SIZE 14,600 square feet (1360 square metres)
RTT Merchandise Mart on Brown Line, Purple Line Express
BUS 16, 37, 41, 44, 56, 61, 125
ACCESS none

Harry Weese & Associates 1990

Harry Weese & Associates 1990

Near North and Streeterville

North Pier

Containing roughly 450,000 square feet of space, this solid red brick and timber warehouse designed by Christian Eckstorm was completed in 1920 after fifteen years of construction. Devoted entirely to wholesale merchandise display, the Pugh Warehouse (after developer James Pugh) was the predecessor of the massive Merchandise Mart and the American Furniture Mart. Conversion of the old warehouse was the initial project of the Cityfront Center complex. The first stage of development for the adaptive reuse of the site involved redirecting the road along Lake Shore Drive to ease automobile access.

North Pier, as it is now called, has been transformed into a trendy, popular retail and office facility. The lower three floors (200,000 square feet) are devoted to small shops and restaurants and the remaining four levels (250,000 square feet) are office lofts. The fact that the floor plates were restricted to 10,800 square feet dictated the size of the boutiques. The entire building is essentially a row of seven inter-connected structures, each 120 x 90 feet. The masterplan for Cityfront Center allocated the site's eastern end for a residential tower. As a result, part of the original 900 foot warehouse was demolished, leaving it just 630 feet long.

Semicircular suspended dark green steel canopies hang above all the entrances on Illinois Street. Windows have been fitted into the old loading dock openings retaining the original dock number stamped on the steel frames. The Ogden Slip elevation has had a white steel and glass curtain wall added, bringing the edge of the building up to the waterfront. Decorative lookouts at either end of the galleria enhance the nautical theme displayed throughout the entire Pier. Outdoor cafés, a wooden boardwalk and docks for tour boats have created a lively location on the north bank of the Chicago River.

Internal circulation in the lower retail portion of the Pier is organised

Booth Hansen & Associates 1990

Booth Hansen & Associates 1990

around a central three-storey rotunda. Escalators at either end of the long layout are fit into curved atriums, visually opening up the space. A thin concrete coat had to be laid over the floor timbers to cut down on noise, but the sandblasted timber frame (it had been covered with white paint) is still visible. The original posts are reinforced with concrete columns with exposed brick capitals. These, along with the remaining heavy timber and brick structure, maximise the rugged maritime tableau.

To emphasise the new and contrast with the existing wood the architects made a point of adding mostly metal elements. Metallic materials are used throughout the interior, perforated or burnished sheet metal, visible clamps, steel mullions and the super original stainless steel floor tiles. All the interior street furniture – lamp posts, rubbish bins and railings – accentuate this industrial vocabulary.

Spots of planned colour enliven the atmosphere; a giant circular lamp suspended from the ceiling in the centre of the building is painted with the bright North Pier motif and then repeated in the floor tiles at the main entrance. This wavy maritime design is also incorporated into some of the metal door handles, a sign of the attention paid to the details of the scheme. The real colour is provided by the crowds who flock to this very popular spot every day.

ADDRESS 435 East Illinois Street (at North McClurg Court)
ASSOCIATE ARCHITECTS/STRUCTURAL ENGINEERS The Austin Company
SIZE 450,000 square feet (41,800 square metres)
COST $20 million
RTT Grand/State on Red Line
BUS 29, 56, 65, 66, 120, 121
ACCESS usual shopping hours

Booth Hansen & Associates 1990

Booth Hansen & Associates 1990

Northwestern University Law School Addition

The existing neo-Gothic building housing the Law School (designed by James Gamble Rogers in 1927) has been joined to a twelve-storey addition by a grey glass and aluminium framed five-storey enclosed atrium. The interior of this recessed atrium juxtaposes the original limestone of the eastern façade and the aluminium and tinted glass walls of the new cascading curtain wall. This central space is dramatically pierced by bridges and a rather grand central staircase that follows the axis of the entryway. The programme for the new building (on an irregular trapezoidal site) encompasses both the national headquarters of the American Bar Association, and facilities for the Law School – an 800-seat auditorium, a library with a 600,000-volume capacity, a moot court room, and three classrooms.

The ABA is the high-rise portion of the extension, physically differentiating it from the four-storey Law School addition. The decorations on the old structure are imitated by drywall buttresses on the new building, just one of many examples of the successful effort made to synthesise elegantly the new with the old. Rigorous attention to detail adds to the finish of the building. The only regrettable feature is the dark reflective glass used on the exterior, which at night is lovely, but somehow during the day does not do justice to the form of the building.

ADDRESS 357 East Chicago Avenue
COST $25 million
SIZE 360,000 square feet (33,000 square metres)
RTT Chicago/State on Red Line
BUS 3, 15, 66, 125, 157
ACCESS public lobby

Near North and Streeterville

Holabird & Root 1984

Holabird & Root 1984

Onterie Center

The playful name Onterie, a combination of Ontario and Erie, the two streets this 60-storey tower sits on, is its most notable feature. The last joint effort of the famous SOM team, architect Bruce Graham and the engineer Fazlur R Khan (responsible for the design of the Sears Tower and the John Hancock Tower), looks positively 1960s'. Using a blend of their innovative structural designs from previous showstopper towers, reinforced concrete bracing is visible on the exterior. This is a bland building with very little to redeem its dated appearance.

Near North and Streeterville

ADDRESS 446–448 East Onterie Street/441 East Erie Street
CLIENT PSM International Corporation
SIZE 1,100,000 square feet (102,000 square metres)
RTT Grand or Chicago on Red Line
BUS 3, 29, 56, 65, 66, 120, 121, 151, 157
ACCESS public lobby

Skidmore, Owings & Merrill, Inc. 1986

Skidmore, Owings & Merrill, Inc. 1986

NBC Tower

Defining the edge of Cityfront Plaza, the National Broadcasting Company Tower was the first structure to be erected at the new 50-acre office, retail and residential complex. This 900,000-square-foot building consists of a 38-storey office tower with a four-storey radio and TV broadcasting facility. Other sites such as in the Illinois Center or behind Quaker Tower were considered by NBC, but Cityfront Center won out.

Begun in 1985, the complex, bordered by Grand Avenue, the Ogden Slip turning basin, the Chicago River, Michigan Avenue and St Clair Street, is an ongoing project. A far more urbanly sensitive scheme than the earlier Illinois Center, the plan appreciates the recreational possibilities of the river.

Before construction of the building started the site had to be rearranged and the necessary infrastructure set up. North Water Street was realigned; services were all re-routed. Circulation and both pedestrian and automobile convenience were important in creating a market for the scheme. An important urban element of NBC is the marble and bronze arcade that runs through the ground floor. Used by the local residents to avoid the freezing Chicago winter, it is part of a plan that hopes to create an interior pedestrian system connecting Columbus Drive to future buildings.

The Cityfront development masterplan, drawn up by Cooper, Eckstut Associates and SOM, set specific architectural guidelines. The building was required to be primarily stone or masonry, measurements for setbacks were specified, and the top 10 per cent of the tower had to be distinctive. The rules for the setbacks were based on 1923 zoning laws, an attempt to be historically contextual. One setback was required at 265 feet above grade to recognise the traditional height of buildings along the Chicago River and a setback at 20 storeys was required where the Tribune Tower has a setback.

Skidmore, Owings & Merrill, Inc. 1989

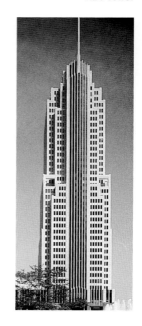

Near North and Streeterville

Skidmore, Owings & Merrill, Inc. 1989

NBC Tower is recognisably derivative of the RCA (now GE) Building at Rockerfeller Center in Manhattan. The series of setbacks, emphasis on elegant verticality and classical materials are a romantic throwback to the skycrapers of the 1920s and 1930s. The neo-Gothic Tribune Tower, built in 1923–1925 by Raymond Hood, also receives homage. Flying buttresses at the 21st floor of the NBC echo those of the Tribune. But the buttresses are functional members, transferring load from the exterior column of the highest portion of the structure to the lower levels outside the column line.

The structural system is post-tensioned, pour-in-place concrete. The curtain wall is of Indiana limestone attached to 2600 precast concrete panels. Patterned precast spandrels alternate with tinted glass, emphasising the verticality of the building. A steel spire soars 130 feet above the roof, making the entire structure rise 602 feet above street level.

Conservative and reactionary, this building is nevertheless graceful, and affable. Perhaps it seems familiar as it is a romantic hybrid of several already traditional façades, or more probably because the building is a nightly TV star as the Channel 5 News icon.

ADDRESS Cityfront Center, 200 East Illinois Street at North Fairbanks Court
CLIENT Tishman Speyer Properties
SIZE 1,098,515 square feet (102,000 square metres)
COST $65 million
RTT Grand/State on Red Line
BUS 2, 3, 11, 29, 56, 65, 66, 120, 121, 145, 146, 147, 151, 157
ACCESS public lobby and arcade

Skidmore, Owings & Merrill, Inc. 1989

Skidmore, Owings & Merrill, Inc. 1989

North Michigan Avenue

900 North Michigan Avenue

North Michigan Avenue has undergone a steady transformation over the last sixty years. In the early part of the century Pine Street (as it was then known) was part of a middle-class residential neighbourhood. The street was broadened into a boulevard and renamed Michigan Avenue as part of Daniel H Burnham's 1909 Grand Plan for the city. Gradually Michigan Avenue became commercial, and by the end of World War 2 this major shopping street was nicknamed Magnificent Mile. Continual commercialisation and upscaling in the 1960s, 1970s and the 1980s occurred as a direct result of changing demographics. Water Tower Place, erected in 1976 (architects Loebl, Schlossman, Dart & Hackl; associate architects C F Murphy & Associates), was the beginning of a new typology along the avenue. This monolithic shopping emporium set the tone for the behemoth vertical malls that dot the Avenue.

Stretching across an entire block, 900 North Michigan Avenue is slightly to the north and on the opposite side of the avenue from Water Tower Place. A more sensitive design than the Tower, the eighth-floor base of its tripartite composition is meant to address the pedestrian, maintaining the low proportions of the street wall. The remaining 58 storeys are set back twice and end in a central arch decorated by four corner pavilions and lanterns. The lanterns are striking against the skyline when lit up at night. Cream limestone, granite and marble are combined with light reflective green glass for a Deco-inspired façade. Decorative vertical striations, large circles and square grids embellish the exterior.

The ubiquitous, supposedly soothing piano player (a baffling must for all posh shopping malls) is audible upon passing through the grandiose two-storey entrance that opens out into a six-storey marble, polished steel and bronze trim atrium. The other atmospheric essential, an elaborate water fountain, dominates the second floor.

Kohn Pedersen Fox 1989

Kohn Pedersen Fox 1989

North Michigan Avenue

The tripartite compositional organisation and geometric theme visible on the exterior has been continued inside. Columns that evolve into light fixtures emphasise verticality and the brass spherical ornaments slightly liven up the restrained, over-pampered environment.

The tower is frequently referred to as the Bloomingdale's Building because Bloomies is the anchor retail store occupying part of the first six levels. The famous New York department store is housed at the rear of the building and luxury boutiques such as Gucci, Henri Bendel, Aquascutum and Charles Jourdan line the atrium. Escalators are strategically placed so that the consumer has to walk by the 100 smaller shops.

Above the retail space is the Four Seasons Hotel, office space and luxury condominium residences on floors 48 through 66. The hotel and private residences have an entrance on Delaware Street while the offices have their own side entrances on Walton Street.

ADDRESS 900 North Michigan Avenue (between East Walton Street and East Delaware Place)
ASSOCIATE ARCHITECTS Perkins & Will
CLIENT JMB Urban Realty
SIZE 2,700,000 square feet (251,000 square metres)
RTT Chicago/State on Red Line
BUS 11, 15, 66, 125, 145, 146, 147, 151
ACCESS public

Kohn Pedersen Fox 1989

North Michigan Avenue

Kohn Pedersen Fox 1989

Barnett Apartment

Planned around a private contemporary art collection, this duplex is the owner's personal gallery and city *pied-à-terre*. The first step in the design process was to photograph and document the collection which includes Mirò aquatints, large Warhol silkscreens, one being the famous 'Marilyn' tapestry, and colourful flag paintings by Ronnie Cutrone. This exciting two-storey open space (there are no conventional rooms) is all angles, curves, soffits, niches, and floating walls bearing paintings and sculptures.

Sited over sixty storeys high in the north-east turret of the 900 North Michigan building and directly across from the John Hancock Tower, the apartment's skyline views are simply spectacular. The city context has been treated as an artwork of equal magnitude and Chicago's grid system is continued in the floor pattern. 5 x 5 foot square floor slabs of highly polished black granite articulated with zinc strips are a luxurious component of the basically neutral palette of the apartment, creating a backdrop for art. From the entranceway, with an alcove housing a sculpture by Beverly Mayeri ('Realignment 1990') the flat unfolds itself, teasing and tantalising with varying views of different artworks set against the spectacular double-height windows. The central focus of the flat is a concrete column (smack in the middle of the atrium) that has been transformed into a replica of the Saturn V rocket. Relevant to the client's profession, aeronautical engineering, this rocket is a structural column supporting a glass and stainless steel elevator. The four-person lift, decked out in industrial checker plate stainless steel flooring, is attached to the cylindrical shaft by a cross-braced steel structure that absorbs all lateral stress. The glass elevator and the overlapping panels of glass in the railings surrounding the upper level allow continued viewing of the paintings and the city. Fragments of the rocket are visible through many of the cutaway partitions.

North Michigan Avenue

Hartshorne Plunkard, Limited 1992

The second level of the apartment has large pneumatic doors pocketed into sculptural walls that slide out to create a bedroom, guestroom and private study. These walls also contain paintings! Even the master bath has been decorated with exquisite hand-made tiles commissioned especially for this project.

The furniture is mostly artwork as well, including a Ron Arad stainless steel number. The home entertainment centre on the first level is contained within a cabinet painted by Neraldo de la Paz to match and act as a continuation of a Kurt Frankenstein moonscape painting, 'Bureaucratic Planet', hung above it.

ADDRESS 132 East Delaware entrance of 900 North Michigan Avenue
STRUCTURAL ENGINEERS Stearn-Joglekar, Limited
SIZE 3500 square feet (325 square metres)
RTT Chicago/State on Red Line
BUS 11, 33, 66, 125, 145, 146, 147, 151, 153
ACCESS none

Hartshorne Plunkard, Limited 1992

North Michigan Avenue

Hartshorne Plunkard, Limited 1992

Oilily

This is a pure geometrical composition. Labelled by the architects as a neo-plastic landscape, two-dimensional patterns on the floor, ceiling and storefront are interlocked with the three-dimensional display furniture.

The playful and colourful exploration of vertical and horizontal linear structure make this small retail space both fun and chic. Shocking pink, yellow, and blue rectilinear volumes create a three-dimensional version of Mondrian's work. Floating cubic display surfaces are set in asymetrical configurations. The solid forms, limited to planes, and round or square shafts are reminiscent of nursery building blocks. The bold colours and textured surfaces complement the wild ethnic motifs of the clothing. Different materials appear in the same colour or pattern, transforming from two to three dimensions and adding another layer of texture.

Narrow vertical shelving for socks, gloves and foldable items offset the horizontal forms. There is no consistent registration of perimeter height, each separate display is at a varying level with its neighbour. The shelves within the cases are all height coordinated and aligned, creating a sense of balance. The epoxy-stabilised floor is an abstract grid that is complemented by the orthogonal lighting fixtures and meshes with the intersecting planes and volumes of the cashwrap and display furniture.

ADDRESS 900 North Michigan Avenue
CLIENT Oilily
SIZE 1600 square feet (150 square metres)
RTT Chicago/State on Red Line
BUS 3, 11, 15, 33, 66, 125, 145, 146, 147, 151, 157
ACCESS open

North Michigan Avenue

Florian-Wierzbowski 1988

`Florian-Wierzbowski 1988

Boogies Diner

Vibrant primary colours, intersecting angular planes, neon signs and industrial vinyl carpet give this clothing shop-cum-eaterie a snappy, snazzy rock'n'roll atmosphere. Bright track lighting sheds an artificial glare on the leather jackets and cowboy boots for sale on the ground level, while diners devour juicy burgers and special curly fries on the upper level. An eclectic mix of vernacular influences dating back to 1950s-style drug store soda fountains and roadside coffee shops, this is the Chicago outlet of the Aspen-based chain. This youthful, super-friendly joint is striving for a clubby mentality. Boogies' own baseball hats signed by music and film celebrities hang in a row above the long lunch counter, indicating the great desirability of being part of the Boogies crowd. Blaring juke box music completes the fun, partytime atmosphere.

North Michigan Avenue

ADDRESS 33 East Oak Street (at North Rush Street)
SIZE 13,000 square feet (1200 square metres)
RTT Chicago/State on Red Line
BUS 11, 15, 22, 33, 36, 66, 125, 145, 146, 147, 151
ACCESS open

Himmel Bonner Architects 1990

North Michigan Avenue

Himmel Bonner Architects 1990

Banana Republic

This free-standing two-storey hut is a romanticised version of a small tropical plantation villa. Robert Stern's first central Chicago commission is this clothing store, suggestive of turn-of-the-century colonial prefabricated metal structures. Stern has created a prototypical make-believe exotic backdrop for this fashionable retailer.

Lead-coated copper panels form the barrel-vaulted roof, and the bronze façade has teak-framed windows complete with pretend tropical shutters. The exterior is beautifully detailed with solid bronze strapping woven round lead-coated copper piers reminiscent of sheaves of bamboo. (Bundles of real dried grasses dot the interior.)

The French colonial settlement motif continues inside. The main focal point is a sophisticated suspended double-return glass and steel staircase, hanging from guyed cables underneath the gabled skylight. The materials are extremely warm and luxurious – leather strapping is woven round the white oak handrail and the laminated glass stairtreads are sandwiched with rice paper. The cross-lashed leather basket-weave theme recurs throughout. Two lacquered particle-board tents laced with steel cable disguise the cash counter areas.

ADDRESS 744 North Michigan Avenue
ARCHITECT OF RECORD Robert W Engel of The Gap
STRUCTURAL ENGINEERS Charles E Pease Associates
SIZE 14,360 square feet (1330 square metres)
RTT Chicago/State on Red Line
BUS 3, 11, 15, 33, 66, 125, 145, 146, 147, 151, 157
ACCESS open

North Michigan Avenue

Robert A M Stern 1991

North Michigan Avenue

Robert A M Stern 1991

City Place

A curiously two-dimensional building, City Place had to be wedged into its narrow corner site. As a result of its narrow profile, broadened width and flat, smooth façade this structure looks as though it was poured into a mold or shaped by a cookie cutter. The thin, wide form required an innovative lateral resisting system with post-tensioned columns to check movement and drift of the building caused by extreme wind loads.

Adjacent to the far gaudier Chicago Place (700 North Michigan Avenue), another complex completed in 1990, City Place is a shiny combination of Imperial red granite and reflective blue glass. Visually divided into three sections, this tripartite organisation – base, shaft and top – is a direct result of programme. The Hyatt Hotel has floors five through twenty-five (special suites are available, decorated in the styles of Mies van der Rohe, Frank Lloyd Wright and Charles Rennie Mackintosh). This area of the façade has punched windows. The top twelve floors, marked by ribbon windows, house the office space. In a reversal of the standard placement, the offices are at the top of the tower and have larger windows. The arch at the top contains the most glass. Its 70-foot diameter barrel vault has a space frame, visible from the sides (if you happen to be forty storeys high), that supports the façade much like a billboard.

ADDRESS 678 North Michigan Avenue (at East Huron Street)
STRUCTURAL ENGINEERS Chris P Stefanos Associates
CLIENT Fifield Realty Corporation and VMS Realty Partners
SIZE 482,000 square feet (44,780 square metres)
RTT Chicago/State on Red Line
BUS 3, 11, 15, 33, 66, 125, 145, 146, 147, 151
ACCESS none

North Michigan Avenue

Loebl, Schlossman & Hackl 1990

Loebl, Schlossman & Hackl 1990

North Michigan Avenue

Sony Gallery

State of the art is the overall image of this sophisticated adult toy store. Punctuated by steel-framed floor-length windows and three navy canopies suspended by cables from the third floor, the four-storey façade is a simple limestone affair. The elegant entrance has a black granite floor inlaid with reflective stainless steel bars. This leads onto bleached oak on which brushed metal pedestals display Sony's latest electronics. All items are available at retail price, but the goal here is for shoppers to experience electronics in a simulated lifestyle setting. A home-theatre display on the first floor demonstrates TV in a pretend living room, complete with Missoni rug and Le Corbusier furniture. A beautiful grey, metal and fabric undulating ceiling wave conceals the system components and audio speakers.

The Boston-based architectural firm Elkus Manfredi chose a neutral palette to highlight and frame the black and white merchandise. The constant video imagery supplies background colour. Semi-transparent perforated metal backdrops separate different product type areas. A central two-way perforated metal and glass staircase passes through the second-floor curved ceiling cutaway, allowing continuous visibility.

North Michigan Avenue

ADDRESS 669 North Michigan Avenue
STRUCTURAL ENGINEERS Weidlinger Associates, Inc.
CLIENT Sony Corporation of America
SIZE 10,000 square feet (930 square metres)
RTT Chicago/State on Red Line
BUS 3, 11, 15, 33, 66, 125, 145, 146, 147, 151
ACCESS open

Elkus Manfredi Architects Limited 1991

North Michigan Avenue

Elkus Manfredi Architects Limited 1991

Niketown

Smack next door to the Sony Gallery is the Nike Museum. A combination of Disneyland meets Smithsonian Institute, this is the sneaker hall of fame, dedicated to the glorification of anything Nike. The basic concept is a three-level pretend-outdoor shopping extravaganza, complete with manhole covers, cement pavement, brick walls, and the piped-in sounds of nature. Far less subtle than the Sony Gallery, although with equal attention to quality of detail, Niketown has a superb element of fun.

The lobby area is the Nike Museum, lined with *Sports Illustrated* covers featuring athletes who endorse Nike. A statue of Michael Jordan and a pair of his autographed shoes accompany plexiglas display cases with information about technological innovations in fitness gear. The amusement park atmosphere is heightened by oversized floats. My favourite display is a video pond, nine television screens installed in the floor and covered with a protective layer of plexiglas that show continuous seascape images.

New, bold and interactive, both the Sony and Nike showcase stores have become consumer cynosures on Magnificent Mile.

ADDRESS 669 North Michigan Avenue at East Erie Street
STRUCTURAL ENGINEERS Chris P Stefanos Associates
SIZE 68,000 square feet (6300 square metres)
CLIENT Nike, Inc.
RTT Grand on Red Line
BUS 3, 11, 15, 33, 125, 145, 146, 147, 151, 157
ACCESS Monday–Friday 10.00–20.00; Saturday 09:30–18.00; Sunday 11.00–18.00

North Michigan Avenue

Gordon Thompson, III and Nike's in-house design team 1992

Gordon Thompson, III and Nike's in-house design team 1992

Terra Museum of American Art

Established in 1980, this collection of American art was originally located in Evanston. The new site, three adjacent buildings, was aquired in 1985. No. 664, the corner building, had its façade cleaned and the interior was transformed from offices to four floors of loft-style galleries. The next-door building has been completely made over. Clad in grey-veined white Vermont marble with a five-storey glass curtain wall insert, this façade is a sophisticated addition to the street. The elegant pavilion elevation is the highlight of the project. At night an elliptical light fixture at the fifth floor makes a spectacular effect.

Past the cosy pale mahogany lobby the building is a big disappointment. The design is baffling: the primary concern seems to be about circulation and not appropiate picture display. Faced with mismatched floor levels and vertically oriented exhibition space, wide, shallow ramps with thin white railings lead to tiny exhibition spaces within No. 666. Obviously inspired by Frank Lloyd Wright's Guggenheim Museum, here the ramps are purely for circulation and do not display any artwork. If No. 670 North Michigan is eventually used, then the ramps can be read as a central circulation point, joining all the buildings, and making a far more sensible scheme.

ADDRESS 666 North Michigan Avenue (at East Erie Street)
STRUCTURAL ENGINEERS Beer Gorski & Graff
CLIENT Ambassador Daniel Terra
SIZE 28,000 square feet (2600 square metres)
COST $3.5 million
RTT Chicago/State on Red Line
BUS 3, 11, 15, 33, 66, 125, 145, 147, 151
ACCESS open

North Michigan Avenue

Booth Hansen & Associates 1987

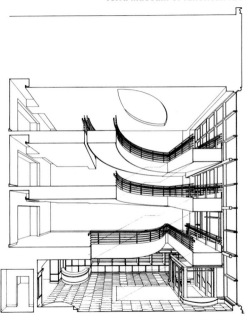

North Michigan Avenue

Booth Hansen & Associates 1987

Crate & Barrel

The national headquarters for this culinary wares and home furnishings store has a sleek exterior expressive of the products it contains. Suggestive of contemporary kitchen machinery, this dynamic flagship building resembles a giant Cuisinart food processor sitting on North Michigan Avenue. A shiny five-storey container with an attached rotunda housing diagonal escalators, this relatively small building stands out against its older and grander masonry-clad neighbours.

Clear glass and glossy white, powder-coated, ribbed aluminium panels create continuous bands of windows on a cube that has a cylindrical attachment. These main forms are literally a crate and a barrel.

The transparency of the glass-enclosed skylit rotunda is a successful commercial ploy. Vertical visibility entices passers-by to look up at the displays on all four retail floors. The entry is adjacent to the rotunda which contains the building's principal means of circulation: escalators. Natural light in the interior of light, knotty pine walls and oak floors creates a relaxed atmosphere. The Midwestern image continues onto the street. The sidewalk is a diamond-patterned smooth-finish concrete that extends from the curb to the store's curtain wall, transforming into oak in the same pattern leading into the interior.

ADDRESS 646 North Michigan Avenue at East Erie Street
STRUCTURAL ENGINEER Chris P Stefanos Associates
SIZE 44,000 square feet (4000 square metres)
RTT Chicago/State or Grand on Red Line AB
BUS 2, 3, 11, 15, 29, 33, 65, 125, 145, 146, 147, 151
ACCESS open

North Michigan Avenue

Solomon Cordwell Buenz & Associates 1990

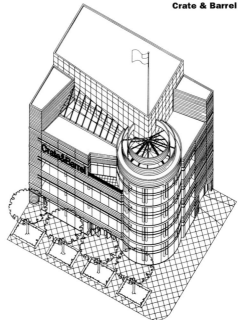

North Michigan Avenue

Solomon Cordwell Buenz & Associates 1990

East Loop

Associates Center

The Associates Center (officially the Stone Container Building) was the ninth collaboration between the architectural firm A Epstein and Sons and New York developers Collins Tuttle & Company. The architects did not have a design team at the time they received the commission for this project. Sheldon Schlegman was appointed project designer for the Associates Center.

The top of the building is oriented towards Burnham Harbor and the Grant Park lakefront, and the base of the building follows the existing grid. Schlegman's main design aim was to create a space where as many of the upper offices as possible could have a view over the lake. The site, the gateway to the Loop, is on the north-west corner of Michigan Avenue and Randolph Street. The split in the middle of the base allows pedestrians a shortcut, an odd amenity as the building is already on the corner. The idea was that the top should make the transition and point eastward, symbolising dynamism and the entrance to Randolph Street, once a Mecca of nightlife. The entranceway is marked by a multicoloured vertical sculpture by Yaacov Agam, 'Communication x9'.

An underground pedestrian walkway, now closed, was designed after a study of existing sewer systems and utilities, under contract with the City of Chicago. The pedway ran under Randolph Street at Michigan Avenue connecting the 150 North Michigan Building to the Illinois Central Railroad Station.

Forty-one storeys, 582 feet overall, the top third of the Associates Center has been canted 45 degrees. Split down the centre, a 'composition of two forces coming together', according to Schlegman, the top half resembles a diamond made up of two sloped triangles. The sloped atrium is faceted in silver reflective insulating glass as is the curtain wall of alternating bands of white polymer-finish spandrel aluminium panels,

A Epstein & Sons 1984

polished stainless steel trim and the reflective glass.

The basic structure is a flat-slab reinforced concrete frame and floors. The central service core has been oriented asymmetrically on a south-east–north-west axis. Although setting the record for perimeter window area per square foot of interior space, the turned core combined with the diagonally angled apex creates some very awkward rooms. These residual spaces must make for difficult interior planning.

Up close, cheap materials and crude detailing exacerbated by the unfortunate white façade make the building clinical and cold. This is, sadly, a no-frills product.

Despite these shortcomings and the fact that much has been written about the building's unflattering proportions (the original plan was intended to be five storeys higher), time and familiarity have made the Associates Center a well-loved element of the skyline. At night, the illuminated diamond with 'Go Bulls' written across its clumsy façade seems like a goofy relative. A well-known albeit clutzy landmark.

ADDRESS 150 North Michigan Avenue
STRUCTURAL ENGINEERS A Epstein & Sons
CLIENT Collins Tuttle & Company
COST $55 million
SIZE 714,000 square feet (66,300 square metres)
RTT Randolph/Wabash on Orange Line. Purple Line Express
BUS 3, 4, 6, 56, 145, 146, 147, 151, 157
ACCESS public lobby and underpass

East Loop

A Epstein & Sons 1984

A Epstein & Sons 1984

Self Park Garage

Heralded by a giant bronze hood ornament gracing its pediment, this twelve-storey grille of a classic touring automobile is snugly wedged in between two early 20th-century skyscrapers. The result of a private competition among three architects, this is a whimsical example of literal symbolism. The alucobond metal-clad exterior with stylised fenders in a baked enamel finish is a turquoise shade taken from the 1957 Chevy colour schedule. The façade has two acrylic prefabricated dome head-lights disguising skylights, bumpers, and black vinyl canopies that resemble tyres, treads and all. The lower two levels are retail and the car park has 199 parking spaces. The finishing touch is the metaphorical license plate signage, SELF PARK.

ADDRESS 60 East Lake Street (between North Wabash and North Michigan Avenues)
ASSOCIATE ARCHITECT Conrad Associates
CLIENT A Ronald Grais and Hersch M Klaff
SIZE 98,000 square feet (9100 square metres)
RTT State/Lake on Brown Line, Orange Line, Purple Line Express
BUS 2, 3, 6, 11, 16, 56, 145, 146, 147, 151, 157
ACCESS public

East Loop

Tigerman Fugman McCurry 1986

Tigerman Fugman McCurry 1986

Athletic Club, Illinois Center

Aside from possessing the tallest (116 feet) indoor climbing wall in Chicago and allegedly having Michael Jordan as a member, the Athletic Club can also claim fame as America's first building designed by Kisho Kurokawa. The gym is a small white structure, almost swallowed up by its neighbours in the dense 83-acre mixed-use development known as the Illinois Center. The Illinois Center is so large that it apparently has several zip codes! Conceived in 1967 by Mies van der Rohe, construction began in 1975 and expected completion is in the late 1990s. Built around an incredibly confusing tri-level street system and incomprehensible pedestrian concourses, the Center is dark and overpowering. Indifferent to Michigan Avenue or the river, the complex is architecturally incoherent. Looming, oppressive tower blocks are packed around gloomy plazas. The light and airy Athletic Club is definitely the highlight.

Only two of the Club's six storeys are visible from Stetson Avenue, the rest are below grade. The exterior is an aluminium and glass curtain wall caged in a white, wide-flange steel framework. The main entrance is at the fifth floor. A whimsical decorative element has been added onto the top level, presumably to draw the eye to the sunken building: steel pedestals support 17-foot kinetic wind sculptures by Osamu Shingu.

ADDRESS 211 North Stetson Avenue
ASSOCIATE ARCHITECTS Fujikawa, Johnson & Associates
STRUCTURAL ENGINEERS CBW Engineers, Inc.
RTT Randolph/Wabash on Brown Line, Purple Line Express, Orange Line
BUS 3, 4, 6, 16, 56, 145, 147, 151, 157
ACCESS private club; try calling

East Loop

Kisho Kurokawa 1990

Kisho Kurokawa 1990

Two Prudential Plaza

At 920 feet, Two Pru is the world's second tallest reinforced concrete building. Similiar in design to Helmut Jahn's Philadelphia skyscraper One Liberty Place (1987) the 63-storey tower has chevron setbacks and a diamond-faceted apex. Its spire seems quite stubby in relation to the vertical length of the building. Sitting between the old Prudential Plaza (a 44-storey Miesian building: Naess & Murphy, 1955), and the very tall Amoco Building (82 storeys, completed 1973: Edward Durrell Stone and Perkins & Will, famous for the accidental loss of its marble cladding), the height of the new Pru makes it appear a logical vertical progression.

The project also involved renovation of the old Pru building, a new 1 acre landscaped public plaza and a five-level parking garage. The two buildings share a common mezzanine and are joined by two five-storey atriums. The award-winning outdoor plaza with two fountains is a popular, flower-filled space. Its concrete structure also functions as the roof for the complex's mechanical equipment.

The new tower is clad in grey and red granite alternating with grey reflective glass. The motif is repeated to death in the entranceway and layered elevator banks. 230 exterior lighting fixtures strategically positioned in the setbacks on the north and south faces and around the chevroned top and spire are illuminated for a dramatic effect at night.

ADDRESS 180 North Stetson Avenue at East Lake Street
SIZE 1,200,000 square feet (111,000 square metres)
STRUCTURAL ENGINEERS CBM Engineers, Inc.
RTT Randolph/Wabash on Brown Line, Orange Line, Purple Line Express
BUS 4, 60
ACCESS public lobby and plaza

Loebl, Schlossman & Hackl 1990

Loebl, Schlossman & Hackl 1990

Leo Burnett Company Headquarters

Structurally quite exciting, this building has a perimeter tube of steel columns on 15-foot centres, with a reinforced cast-in-place concrete service core and trusses supporting the floors. This enables a column-free span of 45 feet. This deep interior space was a requirement for the major tenant, Chicago's largest advertising firm.

Essentially a steel structure with a thin cladding of stone, the building gives the impression of a 50-storey skyscraper wearing an unflattering plaid suit. The granite checkerboard pattern covering the entire height of this free-standing tower destroys its verticality, visually shortening and broadening the building. Three cornice levels continue the pattern, and imitate the base. Three different treatments, thermal stippling, polishing, or honing, were given to the green granite to create a pattern in the building's veneer. Corners, edges and the base of the building are polished granite and the tick-tack-toe pattern of the stuck-on pilasters is outlined alternately by honed and stippled stone. The deeply recessed windows are of dark reflecting glass, adding to the ominous effect.

The overdone pink marble lobby has an incongruous sculpture by John Chamberlain that celebrates materials in a way the building nullifies.

ADDRESS 35 West Wacker Drive at North Dearborn Street
STRUCTURAL ENGINEERS Cohen Barreto Marchertas, Inc.
COST $100 million
SIZE 1,460,000 square feet (135,640 square metres)
RTT State/Lake on Brown Line, Orange Line, Purple Line Express, Clark/Lake on Blue Line, Washington on Red Line
BUS 2, 6, 11, 15, 16, 22, 24, 29, 36, 44, 62, 62 Express, 99, 99M, 125, 146, 162, 164
ACCESS public lobby

East Loop

Kevin Roche-John Dinkeloo & Associates 1989

Kevin Roche-John Dinkeloo & Associates 1989

R R Donnelley Building

From a distance this prominent skyscraper appears amusing but the closer one gets the less funny the pun seems. In fact my final impression is of bewilderment: what is the joke? Spaniard Ricardo Bofill directed the design and DeStefano & Partners were the architects for this 50-storey office tower. Categorised as Modern Classicism, the building is not popular amongst the architectural profession, being jeered at as everything from fascist to trivial and silly!

Apparently meant to be a giant column recalling Giotto's campanile in Florence Cathedral, Bofill wanted his tower to 'reestablish a dialogue between the classicism of stone and the high-tech of glass'. Portuguese white granite abstracted pilasters, arches and entablatures appear to be wallpapered onto the façade. Silver reflective glass windows exacerbate the building's shiny, unreal impression. The patina-green roof inspired by Classical temple proportions sticks to the trend of nighttime illumination.

The self-important base is 42 feet high and houses a grandly proportioned atrium. Giant white marble twisted candy sculptures by Bofill sit alongside a beautiful Tapies and sculptures by Xavier Còrbero in the richly marbled lobby. Dramatic elliptical chandeliers hang from the white oak ceiling.

ADDRESS 77 West Wacker Drive
SUPERVISING ARCHITECTS DeStefano & Partners
STRUCTURAL ENGINEERS Cohen Barreto Marchertas, Inc.
RTT State/Lake on Brown Line, Orange Line, Purple Line Express, Clark/Lake on Blue Line, Washington on Red Line
BUS 2, 6, 11, 15, 16, 22, 24, 29, 36, 44, 62, 62 Express, 99, 99M, 125, 146, 162, 164
ACCESS public lobby

Ricardo Bofill Taller d'Arquitectura 1992

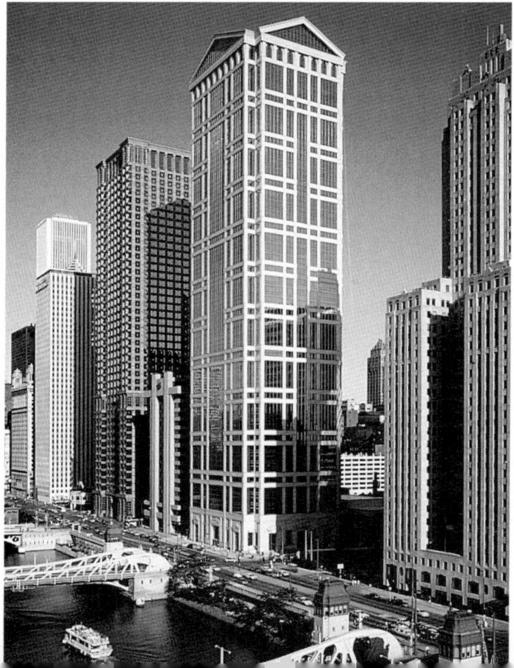

Chicago Title & Trust Center

Part of a two-phase project, the second planned tower of this scheme has been postponed because much of the existing tower is still vacant.

Tall and white, the completed portion of the scheme is a 55-storey monolith that gives the impression that someone got overexcited and went wild with decorating ideas. Ornaments have been stuck all over the façade in a decidely haphazard fashion – there is far too much icing on this vertical cake. Although well constructed and detailed, excessive varieties of signage, patterning, materials (the main lobby alone is faced with three types of marble) and styles combined with confusing asymetrical planes at the apex generate an uncomfortable restless feeling. The exterior, clad in sterile white marble, glass and metal has (off-putting) separate entrances that appear lopsided because they are on different levels and have completely contrary canopies.

The top of the building is ornamented by three sculptural glass and metal pylons. Extended from a 70 foot wide aluminium shaft attached to the tower's western façade are steel bridges that brace the three pylon embellishments. Irregular, overdesigned, and as described in the *Chicago Tribune* (by Blair Kamin), '… there's simply too much going on …'.

ADDRESS 161–171 North Clark Street
CLIENT The Linpro Company
SIZE 2,300,000 square feet (213,700 square metres)
RTT Clark/Lake on Brown Line, Orange Line, Purple Line Express
BUS 16, 22, 24, 36, 42, 44, 62, 135, 136, 156
ACCESS public lobby

East Loop

Kohn Pedersen Fox 1992

Kohn Pedersen Fox 1992

East Loop

Thompson Center

Commissioned by Republican Governor James R Thompson and recently renamed in his honour, this controversial building was originally known as The State of Illinois Center. The anchor project for a 30-acre redevelopment plan to rebuild the Central Business District in the North Loop area, the idea was to gather together 56 different state agencies into one central building. Three thousand state employees are housed in this mixed-use facility, with a million square feet devoted to government offices and 150,000 square feet of commercial space. The inclusion of shops and galleries is intended to bring people in who do not need to renew their driver's license or sort out a tax formality.

The Thompson Center takes up an entire street block. Its unconventional massing basically consists of a low rectangular box with one curved inwardly stepped façade and a diagonally truncated glass cylinder projecting above. This rejection of orthogonal order breaks up the downtown Cartesian grid, diverging from the expected rectilinearity of the rest of Chicago. Although a definite landmark and tourist magnet, the Thompson Center has an uncomfortable and indecisive appearance. The abstract Jean Dubuffet sculpture, 'Monument with Standing Beast', standing on the corner of Randolph and Clark, proclaims pride in its own amorphic form, pointedly mocking the heavy glittery wedge it is meant to complement. The building's bulkiness is exacerbated by its vertically striped polychromatic and mirrored glass skin. Silicone glazing was originally intended, eliminating the need for mullions, but the story has it that the contractors were scared of the possible liabilities. Instead a 2 foot 6 inch vertical division governs alternating strips of reflective glass vision panels and opaque coloured glass panels on the north, east and west façades. The vast heavily lined glass exterior initially caused numerous problems with extreme interior temperature fluctuations.

Murphy/Jahn 1985

Murphy/Jahn 1985

For me, the overriding, far more serious difficulty with this building is that Helmut Jahn's well-intentioned concepts about the reinvention of public space have not survived translation into a built structure. The link between idea and execution has not been successful. References to the centrality of government and the importance of openness in the central piazza-style atrium are diluted by the lack of appreciation for detailing and materials throughout. There has been an enormous amount of understandable criticism concerning the tacky shades of symbolic red, white, and blue that were chosen. Salmon, silver, and powder blue immediately date and cheapen the building. The constantly moving kaleidoscope that one encounters upon entering the atrium is dominated by these trivialising colours topped off by orange structural steel beams that criss-cross the front façade and the roof. All of this, combined with the exposed mechanics of the escalators, mirrored panels and the spinning, geometric rosette-motif patterned marble and granite floor, creates instant vertigo. Perhaps the building succeeds on the level that it is a realistic representation of the merry-go round chaos of bureaucracy – truth in architecture!

ADDRESS bounded by North Clark, North LaSalle, West Lake and West Randolph Streets
ASSOCIATE ARCHITECTS Lester B Knight & Associates
SIZE 1,930,000 square feet gross (179,000 square metres)
CLIENT State of Illinois Capital Development Board
COST $172 million
RTT Clark/Lake on Brown Line, Blue Line, Orange Line, Purple Line Express
BUS 22, 24, 42, 135, 136, 156
ACCESS public

Murphy/Jahn 1985

Murphy/Jahn 1985

Vivere

Layers of sensual spirals in a soft rusty palette create a magical neo-Baroque ambience in this lovingly renovated restaurant. Each romantic surface and voluptuous object – tableware, door handles, chairs, walls, tables – has been custom-designed by the hotshot designer Jordan Mozer. Involved at every level and stage of design and execution, Mozer has been called a throwback to the days of the masterbuilder. Working directly with artisans, he had practically everything in Vivere handmade. His method of working sometimes consists of blowing-up freehand drawings to life-size and having craftsman build directly from these.

The omnipresent spiral motif was inspired by a detail in the original space (known as the Florentine Room), and seized upon as representative of Italian Baroque architecture. This was pertinent because, as the third of three restaurants housed in one building, called Italian Village, Vivere serves delicious though eclectic, gourmet, regional and seasonal Italian cuisine, and has a renowned wine list. The spiral metaphorically represents the genealogical history of the restaurant's ownership, having been founded three generations ago in 1927 by an Italian immigrant, handed down to his children and currently run by their grandchildren.

This super-meaningful helix is evident everywhere in the long, narrow, split-level space. A curvy iron entry gazebo, behind the large mahogany front door, paves the way for endless twisty, bulgy forms. 13-foot, copper, internally illuminated corkscrews descend like fat slinky toys from the ceiling. In the centre of the rear main room an 8-foot-wide chandelier supposedly fabricated by an aeroplane nose-cone company is inlaid with a leaded glass whorl. The chairs, bar stools and booths finish in twists, and the bar itself is a spiral.

These ripe, organic shapes are complemented by rich surfaces on the walls, mosaic floors, and stained-glass panels. Silk drapery hangs above

Jordan Mozer & Associates 1990

Jordan Mozer & Associates 1990

narrow mirrors on textured walls that have had streaks of different coloured plaster applied with a cake icer. The snailshell-shaped lighting fixtures are particularly wonderful, made of handblown glass set in copper.

Drama and theatricality are appropriate here; the restaurant has always been patronised by opera stars and fans from the nearby Lyric Opera.

ADDRESS 71 West Monroe Street (between South Dearborn and South Clark Streets)
SIZE 5500 square feet (510 square metres)
COST $980,000
CLIENT the Capitanini Family
RTT Monroe on Red Line, Blue Line
BUS 1, 7, 22, 24, 36, 42, 60, 62, 126, 129, 130, 151
ACCESS Monday–Saturday 11.00–14.30, 17.00–21.45

Jordan Mozer & Associates 1990

Jordan Mozer & Associates 1990

Ralph H Metcalfe Federal Center

A competition for this federal project was held in 1988 among architect/developer/contractor teams. This is the first building constructed under the auspices of a new programme run by the General Service Administration, the government agency responsible for property management. The Design Build programme is economically advantageous as private developers become responsible for delivering an entire package at a fixed cost. Siting, design, construction, long-term financing, and guaranteed occupancy were all part of the specifications. An unusual ownership contract is involved as well. After thirty years of paying regular monthly rent the government gets full ownership.

The interesting twist to this arrangement was that the siting of the building was part of the competitive scheme. Property rights narrowed the field down, and it was probably due to luck, not a masterplan, that the building ended up adjacent to three other federal buildings, in the Chicago Federal Center, creating a small centralised governmental enclave. The winning scheme was designed to complement the Miesian structures surrounding it. The Post Office and the nearby Dirksen and Klucynski Buildings were begun in 1961 by Mies van der Rohe and completed by 1974.

The new building is named after US representative Ralph Metcalfe (also at one time an Olympic star) and is home to the Environmental Protection Agency, US Department of Agriculture, Social Security Administration and the Department of Housing and Urban Development.

Twenty-seven storeys with a two-storey annexe, this tall, rectangular building has 600,000 square feet of office space. The bustle houses amenities such as a staff cafeteria, a daycare centre, a health club and a 9000 square foot conference centre. Serious and dignified, this understated tower has a 27-foot-high lobby similar to its neighbours. The curtain wall

Fujikawa, Johnson & Associates 1991

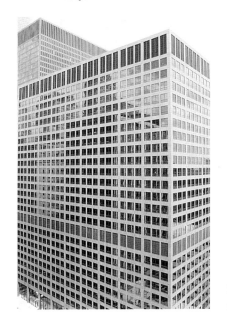

Fujikawa, Johnson & Associates 1991

and structural columns are clad in black-grey thermal finish granite creating a sombre Modernist ambience. Structurally a straightforward poured-in-place reinforced concrete beam/slab system using post-tensioning tendons in the east–west direction, this building had a couple of unusual technical requirements. The type of soil the building sits on required that the caissons had to be very wide in diameter (some are 9 feet across) under the high-rise section of the building. The need for computers and sophisticated communication equipment required an exorbitant number of power outlets. The electrified floordeck system has one outlet per 90 square feet as compared to the average of one per 175 square feet.

In summer 1993 a Frank Stella sculpture commissioned by the GSA as part of their art in architecture series (under the national scheme a half per cent of construction cost is set aside for art) was installed. This 118-foot-high steel and aluminium work, 'The Town-Ho's Story', is one in a series of 135 different sculptures, each based on a chapter in *Moby Dick*.

ADDRESS 77 West Jackson Boulevard
STRUCTURAL ENGINEER Cohen Barreto Marchertas, Inc.
CLIENT US General Services Administration and Stein & Company Federal Center, Inc.
COST $95 million
SIZE 800,000 square feet (74,300 square metres)
RTT Jackson/State on Red Line, Jackson/Dearborn on Blue Line, La Salle/Van Buren on Brown Line, Orange Line, Purple Line Express
BUS 1, 7, 22, 24, 42 60, 62, 126, 129, 130, 151
ACCESS public lobby

East Loop

Fujikawa, Johnson & Associates 1991

Fujikawa, Johnson & Associates 1991

Daniel F and Ada I Rice Building

It is easy to miss the austere historicist exterior of this addition to the Art Institute. The Spartan Indiana-limestone-clad façade with mere suggestions of ornament and practically no windows is neo-Classical. Hiding at the south corner of the original Beaux-Arts building, the extension is overshadowed by the Illinois Central Railroad tracks. The main entrance is through the grand old building so the Rice addition's public face (the south façade) is only used as an occasional exit.

The project included renovation of the existing building (completed in 1987) and relocation of the museum's central cooling tower. The three-storey addition provides exhibition and storage space. The internal entrance to the new galleries is on a cross-axis with the original building. The formality of the overall design is emphasised by the serene colours used throughout. The first floor is focused around an elegant, unashamedly Classical, two-storey skylit sculpture court framed by colonnades. Axial views allow peeks into the surrounding American art galleries.

The structural layout has repeatedly been described as a 'Thermos bottle' design. Services have been sandwiched into thin spaces running along the inside perimeters of the building, creating a passive vapour barrier. With incredible respect for its contents, this extension has been very literally treated as a container for the precious objects within.

ADDRESS Michigan Avenue at Adams Street
STRUCTURAL ENGINEERS Cohen Barreto Marchertas, Inc.
SIZE 130,000 square feet (12,000 square metres)
RTT Adams/Wabash on Brown Line, Orange Line, Purple line Express
BUS 1, 3, 4, 6, 7, 14, 60, 126, 127, 129, 145, 147, 151
ACCESS Monday, Wednesday, Friday 10.30–16.30, Tuesday, 10.30–20.00, Saturday 10.00–17.00, Sunday 12.00–17.00

East Loop

Hammond, Beeby & Babka 1988

Hammond, Beeby & Babka 1988

A mixture of traditional Japanese architecture and geometric minimalism characterises Tadao Ando's first project in America. This signature space is the last room in the recently renovated 16,500 square foot Chinese, Japanese, and Korean wing of the Art Institute.

Access is through glass doors, necessary for proper temperature and humidity control. A symmetrical forest of sixteen free-standing oil-stained oak columns, a foot square and 10 feet high, forms a grid directly in front of the entrance. According to Ando, '… the pillars obstruct the viewer's gaze and yet help to suggest depth and resonance of the space. As the visitor moves through this space, the static pillars change their relationships. At times the pillars overlap and unite'.

The display cases containing the screens and ancient ash-glazed stoneware jars seem oddly placed, winding in an L formation along the back and right side walls. They are actually placed to make a point. Physical metaphors for the expansion of space, the panels' purpose is the division of space for privacy yet the art they sport suggests spatial depth.

ADDRESS The Art Institute of Chicago, South Michigan Avenue at East Adams Street
ASSOCIATED ARCHITECTS Cone Kalb Wonderlick
STRUCTURAL ENGINEERS Knight Architects Engineers Planners, Inc.
SIZE 1850 square feet (172 square metres)
RTT Adams/Wabash on Brown Line, Orange Line, Purple Line Express
BUS 1, 3, 4, 6, 7, 14, 60, 126, 127, 145, 147, 151
ACCESS Monday, Wednesday–Friday 10.30–16.30; Tuesday 10.30–20.00; Saturday 10.00–17.00 Sunday and holidays 12.00–17.00

East Loop

Tadao Ando Architect & Associates 1992

East Loop

Tadao Ando Architect & Associates 1992

Harold Washington Library

Love it or hate it, Chicago's first central library is dichotomous in many respects, not the least in the reaction it elicits on first viewing. The largest municipal library in America it is one of the largest public libraries in the world, second only to the British Library in London. Controversial from its inception, a design/build competition (financed by a bond issue), relatively rare in the States, was held in 1988 to decide the architect. Drawings by six teams were exhibited and the public became involved.

Named after the city's first black mayor, it is significant that one of the most important buildings to be erected in Chicago in the early 1990s is a civic space. The library houses approximately 2,000,000 circulating volumes and has ten floors, each devoted to specific topics. The programme includes an orientation theatre, language-learning centre, 385-seat auditorium, video theatre, public restaurant and a bookstore.

While this is all very good, once again the coin has two sides. It is very reassuring that a repository for books, a sanctuary in fact, exists in a post-urban environment, but has any thought been given to the nature of a contemporary library, or of a library for the future? Information technology is changing so rapidly that the question must be posed: is such a retrograde building (architecturally and functionally) appropriate? Need a library be a memorial?

The building has inspired extreme criticism leaning in all possible directions. Called everything from a monstrous behemoth to the best civic building in 60 years, the most important critic is the public and the overwhelming reaction seems to be one of enthusiasm.

There is no mistaking this as a bold and brawny monolithic public building. The Beaux-Arts/neo-Classical exterior is massive in scale, the rusticated granite base looming powerfully (verging on the threatening) over passers-by. Monumentally heavy walls are emphasised and exag-

Hammond, Beeby & Babka 1991–1993

Hammond, Beeby & Babka 1991–1993

gerated by recessed five-storey arched openings containing windows of several floors. Durable deep red brick (the familiar colour enhances the solid image) faces the building from the third floor up, the floor levels marked externally by horizontal bands of cast stone.

Decoration is an intrinsic part of the library's vocabulary. The façade is covered with stone iconography based on historical Chicago themes. Reminiscent of Greek temples, the ornament starts as an intertwined chain-patterned strip (guilloche) around the base, with foliated scroll-work above. Huge cast-stone corn stalks, oak leaves, swords and shields, Ceres (a popular Chicago theme also adorning the 1930 Board of Trade Building), and other harvest symbols cover the exterior, surrounding 22 allegorical medallions on the seventh floor. A glass curtain wall emerges at the ninth floor, forming massive pediments topped with seven over-scaled aluminium gargoyles. Designed and sculpted by Kent Bloomer and Raymond Kaskey, these ornaments are breathtaking from far away but seem plastic and Disney-like up close.

There is something oppressive about the massive over-scaling of this building and its ornaments. It is as though the gigantic owls on the roof could swoop down and gobble up the tiny mortals at the structure's base.

ADDRESS 400 South State Street between West Congress and Van Buren
ASSOCIATE ARCHITECTS A Epstein & Sons
COST $144 million
SIZE 760,000 square feet (70,600 square metres)
RTT Jackson/State on Red Line
BUS 2, 6, 11, 15, 29, 36, 44, 62, 62 Express, 99, 99M, 146, 162, 164
ACCESS Tuesday to Thursday 09.00–19.00, Friday to Saturday 09.00–17.00

East Loop

Hammond, Beeby & Babka 1991–1993

Hammond, Beeby & Babka 1991–1993

West Loop

One Financial Place

The centrepiece of a new trio of financial structures that is physically and electronically linked with the gorgeous Art Deco Chicago Board of Trade. State-of-the-art provisions have been made to distribute necessary data/telecommunications services vertically and horizontally throughout the complex.

This 39-storey structural steel tower clad in Imperial red granite with bronze tinted vision glass sits on what used to be the train shed and railroad tracks of the LaSalle Street Station. An integral part of the complex is an obscurely placed plaza with a fountain and bronze horse sculpture by Ludovico de Luigi, a tribute to the piazza of all piazzas – St Mark's in Venice - with which this plaza has nothing in common except air.

ADDRESS 440 South LaSalle Street
CLIENT Financial Place Partnership
COST $62 million
SIZE 1,147,350 square feet
(106,600 square metres)
RTT La Salle Van Buren on Brown Line,
Orange Line, Purple Line Express
BUS 11, 37, 135, 136, 156
ACCESS public lobby and plaza

West Loop

Skidmore, Owings & Merrill, Inc. 1985

West Loop

Skidmore, Owings & Merrill, Inc. 1985

Chicago Board Options Exchange

Affectionately called the CBOE amongst insiders, this building houses the growing facilities of The Chicago Board of Trade. Lined by sidewalk arcades, this ten-storey box secretively shelters a 44,000-square-foot trading floor and another columnless, capacious floor to be used for future expansion. An Exchange Bridge (added in 1987) links the Chicago Board of Trade with the CBOE, making the biggest adjacent trading floor area in the United States. This exposed steel truss supported by a large pier serves to regulate interior circulation.

Located on one side of One Financial Place, the financial complex is completed by a third structure, the Midwest Stock Exchange, flanking the other side of One Financial Place. All three buildings are clad in red granite and have bronze-tinted windows although the CBOE has a negligible number of windows, hence the private, furtive effect.

ADDRESS 141 West Van Buren Street
CLIENT One Financial Place Partnership
SIZE 348,000 square feet (32,300 square metres)
RTT La Salle Van Buren on Brown Line, Orange Line, Purple Line Express
BUS 41, 60, 157
ACCESS none

West Loop

Skidmore, Owings & Merrill, Inc. 1985

West Loop

Skidmore, Owings & Merrill, Inc. 1985

Savings of America Tower

A curved grey-tinted glass bay extending over LaSalle Street is topped by an extraordinary projecting cantilevered trellis. This architectural element then transforms into a ladder and finally culminates in a wall sitting on the quarter vault pinnacle. This adds to the asymmetrically arranged façade of this narrow 40-storey building.

A fine example of texture, materials and geometrical form, this is one of Helmut Jahn's finest buildings. The curved entrance gallery, also placed off centre, has a wonderful 20 x 50 foot curved mosaic, 'Flight of Daedulus and Icarus' (by Roger Brown) flying above. Ingredients intrinsic to the building's design are echoed in the mural. Clearly some collaboration between artist and architect occurred, and it is refreshing to see artwork incorporated in a building's design.

ADDRESS 120 North LaSalle Street
CLIENT Ahmanson Commercial Development, Mitsui & Co.
STRUCTURAL ENGINEERS Martin/Lam, Inc.
SIZE 400,000 square feet (37,000 square metres)
COST $48 million
RTT Randolph/Wells on Brown Line, Orange Line, Purple Line Express, Washington on Blue Line
BUS 20, 23, 56, 127, 131, 135, 136, 156, 157
ACCESS public lobby

West Loop

Murphy/Jahn 1991

Murphy/Jahn 1991

Holabird & Root Offices

Founded in 1880, Holabird & Root is one of the oldest architectural firms in America. Originally established as Holabird & Roche, the partnership was handed down to the next generation in the late 1920s. The firm's title was altered when Holabird's son John was joined by John Root, Jr, whose own father had been Daniel Burnham's partner. They had met while finishing their studies at the Ecole des Beaux Arts in Paris and returned to Chicago to take over the well-established firm. The founding designers were known for their powerful Chicago School buildings. Amongst their definitive steel-frame edifices are the McClurg and Old Colony buildings. The younger partners became famous for such spectacular Art Deco buildings as the Chicago Board of Trade and the Palmolive Building, and civic institutions such as the magnificent Soldier Field.

The present partners recently decided to renovate their own offices. Based in a 70-year old courtyard building, their dominant aim was to make full use of the central light court. The clever solution was to insert a steel and glass bridge diagonally spanning this open area. Internal circulation could be reorganised and opened up by functional use of the light court. This dynamic hanging walkway leads across from the elevator exit to the walled-in reception area. As the office plan is an L, those afraid of heights can take the longer route around the bridge.

Structurally, the bridge floor is hung from its roof structure and outrigger-type brackets minimise its load on the existing concrete frame. These brackets are tied to two concrete columns with steel jackets. The actual construction involved shop-fabricated members being lifted by crane into the office through a window, put together and pulled across the light court by a winch and then hung in position.

An industrial quality defines the drafting and work areas. The exposed mechanical services, electrical ducts and power drops are intentional

West Loop

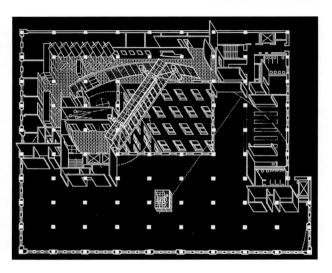

Holabird & Root 1992

references to what the firm refers to as the machine aesthetic. The administrative area is more refined, with slate floors and curving glass walls. Executive spaces are separated by fritted glass partitions. Six pivoting, perforated metal screens rotate to serve a double function as display panels and space dividers, creating a semi-private conference space. The meeting room opposite has a wonderful, curved, heavy sliding door on a giant track. This is the slide show room and affords greater privacy.

In 1992 the firm won an Honor Award (Divine Detail category) for the bridge and a Citation of Merit for the whole scheme from the Chicago Chapter of the American Institute of Architects.

ADDRESS 300 West Adams Street
STRUCTURAL ENGINEERS David Ekstrom
CLIENT Holabird & Root
SIZE 22,500 square feet (2100 square metres)
RTT Quincy/Wells on Brown Line, Orange Line, Purple Line Express
BUS 1, 7, 37, 60, 61, 126, 129, 130, 135, 136, 156
ACCESS on request

West Loop

Holabird & Root 1992

Holabird & Root 1992

190 South La Salle Street

Philip Johnson and John Burgee's only project in Chicago stands on the corner of the La Salle Street canyon in the heart of the financial district. Classified as both Postmodern and historicist, this 40-storey tower is a study in formal pastiche. Elegant and graceful, it has often been criticised as pretentious. Inspiration clearly came from Burnham & Root's 1886 Rookery building. The overall design is loosely based on John W Root's Masonic Temple, built in 1892 and demolished in 1939.

Like two completely different buildings, the top of 190 South La Salle differs drastically from the bottom. The five-storey rusticated base is built of red granite and is a direct reference to the Rookery. The 35-storey tower of pink granite and tinted glass is much lighter and more refined. The roof, reminiscent of the Masonic Temple, has six copper-clad, aluminium-crested gables housing a law library and reading room. Set on each side of the gables are whimsical concrete balls, evidence of Johnson's penchant for paraphrasing historical references. The 50-foot-high entrance arch leads into an over-scaled barrel-vaulted lobby. Even the elevator cabs have goldleaf-covered vaulted ceilings and marble floors! Huge bronze chandeliers hang above the black and white marble checkerboard floor, dwarfing a sculpture by Anthony Caro, 'Chicago Fugue'.

ADDRESS 190 South La Salle Street
ASSOCIATE ARCHITECT Shaw & Associates, Inc.
SIZE 9,000,000 square feet (836,100 square metres)
STRUCTURAL ENGINEERS Cohen Barreto Marchertas, Inc.
RTT Quincy/Wells or LaSalle Van Buren on Brown Line, Orange Line, La Sale/Congress on Blue Line
BUS 1, 7, 2 2, 24, 37, 42, 60, 65, 62 local, 126, 135, 136, 156
ACCESS public lobby

West Loop

John Burgee Architects with Philip Johnson 1987

West Loop

John Burgee Architects with Philip Johnson 1987

Chemical Plaza

The original 1912 structure standing on this LaSalle Boulevard site was the Otis building designed by Holabird & Roche. The Classical Revival granite and terracotta base was preserved in order to continue the traditional streetscape and to allow the new structure to retain a relationship with its neighbours. Adding a 33-storey office building on top, the Canadian firm Moriyama & Teshima left the north and east walls of the four bottom storeys intact. The load of the new building's columns was simply transferred to some of the large caissons of the original building.

There are only two demarcations of the changeover between old and new. The tower glazing directly above the base is set back slightly and a semicircular seven-storey lobby has been inserted behind the historic façade. This creates a transitional space as one passes through the old thick walls and progresses into the newer lobby. To accommodate as many corner offices as possible (ten per floor) the north-west and south-west corners are stepped back in phases.

An otherwise unremarkable office building, the cobalt blue painted frame, bright green detailing and blue-silver tinted windows make this tower block noticeable, inappropriate and out of place.

ADDRESS 10 South LaSalle Street
ASSOCIATE ARCHITECTS Holabird & Root
STRUCTURAL ENGINEERS Cohen Barreto Marchertas, Inc.
CLIENT Fidinam (USA), Inc.
COST $43 million
SIZE 844,000 square feet (78,400 square metres)
RTT Quincy/Wells on Brown Line, Orange Line, Purple Line Express
BUS 14, 20, 23, 56, 127, 131, 135, 136, 156, 157
ACCESS public lobby

West Loop

Moriyama & Teshima Architects 1986

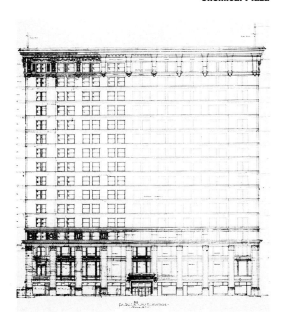

West Loop

Moriyama & Teshima Architects 1986

Helene Curtis Corporate Headquarters

At the junction of the Wells Avenue Bridge and the north bank of the Chicago River, a 1912 warehouse designed by L Gustav Hallberg has been renovated to become home to America's second largest cosmetic manufacturers. The company was founded in Chicago in 1927 and still maintains its world headquarters in the windy city. The extensive overhaul of the 168,000-square-foot building has been jokingly dubbed a facelift or beauty makeover by many architectural critics. And a most successful makeover at that!

The rehab began with the gutting of the interior, leaving only the brick shell, support columns and stair tower. A floor was added at the top, making the structure 10 storeys tall, emerging as a green glass cylinder surrounded by two glass squares capping the building. The glass is a sumptuous green and consistent from the bottom of the structure up so it seems as though the fenestrations at the top have broken free from their brick constraints. The flags waving from the roof slam home the nautical theme. This tenth floor is a two-storey boardroom surrounded by smaller executive spaces. The oval conference room, complete with Saarinen furniture, is serene and posh. The entire interior is geared towards promoting an ambience of individual importance. Bleached oak-panelled workstations throughout the offices have been designed according to user needs. The monotony of the ceiling is alleviated by puffs of acoustical tiles.

ADDRESS 325 North Wells Street
SIZE 163,000 square feet (15,000 square metres)
COST $13 million
RTT Merchandise Mart on Brown Line, Purple Line Express
BUS 37, 41, 44, 61, 125
ACCESS public lobby

West Loop

Booth Hansen & Associates 1984

222 North La Salle Street Addition

An elegant renovation and limestone clad addition to the Builders' Building erected in 1927, designed by Graham, Anderson, Probst & White. The addition on the western side of the existing building retains the proportions and compositional principles of the existing façade.

Significant energy and expense has been spent on redesigning the entryway. A three-storey, three-bay-wide loggia leads to a two-storey lobby that terminates at the restored rotunda. This four-storey atrium, the link between the old and new structures, is artificially backlit, and redecorated in the original 1927 colour scheme complete with gold-leaf detailing. A grand staircase is the central focus of the space as the elevators have been moved to the addition. Wooden spandrels replace the decaying decorative iron spandrels and a new marble floor extending into the addition (a further connection between the two structures) replaces the previous terrazzo. The entire roof has been replaced by a four-storey glass sloped penthouse, visually connecting the two buildings.

ADDRESS 222 North LaSalle Street
CLIENT Tishman Speyer Properties
SIZE 1,030,000 square feet (96,000 square metres)
COST $46,750,000
RTT Clark/Lake on Blue Line, Brown Line, Orange Line, Purple Line Express
BUS 135, 136, 156
ACCESS public lobby

West Loop

Skidmore, Owings & Merrill, Inc. 1986

Skidmore, Owings & Merrill, Inc. 1986

181 West Madison Street

Vertical and vast describe Cesar Pelli's only Chicago tower. A seemingly straightforward glass (and granite-clad pier) curtain wall has been subtly modified to add dimensionality. Vertical ribs of granite express the 5- foot interior floor modules, and metal accent mullions (set slightly away from the windows) are centred between the vertical ribs, reinforcing the tower's verticality. The piers end in metal finials 9 inches from the top of the glass line and are meant to reflect sunlight and add height when lit at night.

The vastness occurs in the interior, a vaulted coffered ceiling lobby preceded by a four-storey glass roofed loggia on the Madison Street front. In the deliberately overscaled five-storey lobby even at lunch hour the space feels deserted and the lone receptionist looks lost amidst miles of white, grey and green marble in this ghost town room.

The developers of Paine Webber Tower, as 181 West Madison is known, Miglin-Beitler and Cesar Pelli & Associates have an extraordinary proposition for another building. A 125-storey tower was planned as the tallest building in the world to be located at the south-west corner of Madison and Wells Streets. Elegant as the model and plans appear, the need for such macho architecture is elusive.

ADDRESS 181 West Madison Street at Wells Street
ASSOCIATE ARCHITECT Shaw & Associates, Inc.
STRUCTURAL ENGINEER Cohen Barreto Marchertas, Inc.
COST $75 million
SIZE 1,000,000 gross square feet (93,000 square metres
RTT Quincy/Wells or Randolph/Wells on Brown Line, Orange Line, Purple Line Express
BUS 20, 23, 37, 56, 61, 127, 131, 157
ACCESS public lobby

West Loop

Cesar Pelli & Associates 1990

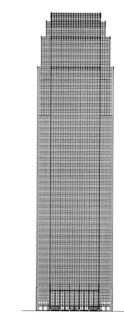

West Loop

Cesar Pelli & Associates 1990

Chiasso

Adjacent to the lobby of the glossy Skidmore, Owings & Merrill 303 Madison Street office tower (completed in 1988) is an amusingly witty store. Packed with trendy designer objects, accessories and toys for the modern executive, the shop points a gently mocking finger at the dead serious building it inhabits.

Conceived as a stage set in the process of either being constructed or disassembled, the shop consists of fragmented forms placed in an unfinished space. Amongst exposed ductwork and an unusually furry ceiling (most likely faux insulation!) only synthetic-faux materials have been used. The 'industrial look' has taken a new twist with exposed standard scaffolding supporting fragments of display tables covered, of course, in faux pigskin laminates.

Faux granite, faux bronze, faux brushed aluminium, faux ebonised oak and even faux paint texture laminates create this anecdotal environment. The contrast between the very serious, shiny, dark, marble lobby and the sleek corporate toys available in the shop is extremely clever.

ADDRESS 303 Madison Street
SIZE 870 square feet (81 square metres)
RTT Quincy/Wells on Brown Line, Orange Line, Purple Line Express
BUS 14, 20, 37, 56, 61, 127, 129, 131, 157
ACCESS open

West Loop

Florian-Wierzbowski 1988

Florian-Wierzbowski 1988

AT&T Corporate Center, USG Building

The lavish foyer of this temple to the telephone is appropriately cathedralesque. Costing approximately $3 million, almost everything in the 40-foot vaulted lobby was custom designed. The skylit central hall covered with marble and exotic woods serves as the connection between the two buildings. The second floor of this hall is part of the building's public space and has restaurants and shops as well as an amazing vista of the vast, richly detailed and beautifully crafted lobby. Marble, gold leaf, and American oak walls are complemented by the elaborately patterned Italian marble floor. Satin finish bronze grilles and feature strips line the ceiling from which three massive chandeliers dangle.

Covering an entire block and almost 900 feet tall, the two buildings together contain over 2.4 million square feet. A combination of Art Deco, Modernism and what some critics call Revivalism, this building has been inspired, like much of architect Adrian Smith's work, by the Tribune Tower and other 1920s' skyscrapers. The tripartite granite façade emphasises verticality. The AT&T building rises 60 storeys and the USG is somewhat smaller at 34 storeys.

An interesting technique was used to pattern the 2600 decorative aluminium panels that separate the windows. Meant to evoke turn-of-the-century ornamental ironwork, imprints were photographed onto each panel, bypassing the more usual stencilling process.

This very prolific firm, SOM, founded in Chicago in 1936 as Skidmore and Owings, has several other recent towers in the Loop worth mentioning. A 28-storey red granite clad, rather petite skyscraper can be found at 225 West Washington Street (1986). One North Franklin (1991) is another Art-Deco corporate pageant and 303 West Madison (1988) has a beautiful stained-glass wall facing Franklin Street. 500 West Monroe (1992) has a dramatic nine-storey base topped by a 36-storey

West Loop

Skidmore, Owings & Merrill, Inc. 1989, 1992

West Loop

Skidmore, Owings & Merrill, Inc. 1989, 1992

series of setbacks and is yet another record holder as the current tallest office tower on the west bank of the Chicago River.

ADDRESS 227 West Monroe Street and 125 South Franklin Street
CLIENT Stein & Co.
COST $250 million and $94 million
SIZE 1,750,000 square feet (162,600 square metres) and 1,100,000 square feet (102,000 square metres)
RTT Quincy/Wells on brown Line, Orange Line; Purple Line Express
BUS 1, 7, 37, 60, 61, 19, 129, 130, 135, 136, 151, 156
ACCESS public lobby

West Loop

Skidmore, Owings & Merrill, Inc. 1989, 1992

Skidmore, Owings & Merrill, Inc. 1989, 1992

311 South Wacker Drive

Another record-breaking building, this 959-foot-tall skyscraper is the world's tallest reinforced-concrete office tower. The first phase in a three-tower development on the South Wacker Drive site, the projected complex (estimated to be 4,000,000 square feet in total) will be focused around the recently built Wintergarden plaza. This is a vast 80-foot barrel-vaulted space intended as a pedestrian hub with pedways linking the building with transportation systems. The skylight corridor is supported by white painted steel rising from granite piers and once the remaining towers are built will unfortunately be hidden from the sun.

The 65-storey tower is clad in a pinky shade of Texas red granite with shiny horizontal strapping increasing in density at the lower levels.

The top of the building is its most extraordinary feature. It has been nicknamed 'White Castle' for the giant (105 feet tall) translucent glass cylinder surrounded by four smaller glass cylinders perched on the 51st floor. Not well liked by the architectural community, the drums, especially when lit at night by 1852 florescent tubes, seem a trifle medieval, and unnecessarily territorial.

ADDRESS 311 South Wacker Drive
ASSOCIATE ARCHITECTS Harwood K Smith & Partners
CLIENT Lincoln Property Company
SIZE 1,400,000 square feet (130,000 square metres)
RTT Quincy/Wells on Brown Line, Orange Line, Purple line Express
BUS 1, 7, 60, 121, 123, 126, 130, 135, 136, 151, 156
ACCESS public lobby

West Loop

Kohn Pedersen Fox 1990

Kohn Pedersen Fox 1990

Chicago Mercantile Exchange

Two 40-storey granite and glass twin office towers stand on either side of the ten-storey Carnelian granite clad structure that houses the 40,000-square-foot trading floor of the project's major tenant. A floor above the trading area also has 30,000 square feet of column-free space, an admirable structural feat. This was achieved by cantilevering a substantial section of the top 34 storeys of the two towers over the low-rise building, allowing loads to be carried to the ground without columns in the trading spaces. Built in two phases, the first tower was in use and the trading floor was occupied by the time the second tower was erected. Fronting the Chicago River (affording spectacular views), the entire structure presents a calm, solid ambience, quite the antithesis of the interior activities.

It is possible to view the trading floor, a fascinating and colourful experience as the different colour coats run and gesticulate frantically. The fourth floor visitors' gallery is reached via a separate elevator shuttle, bypassing the many escalators carrying runners and traders back and forth.

ADDRESS 10 and 30 South Wacker Drive
STRUCTURAL ENGINEERS Alfred Benesch & Co.
CLIENT Metropolitan Structures/JMB Urban Realty
COST $350 million
RTT Quincy/Wells or Randolph/Wells on Brown, Orange, Purple Lines
BUS 20, 23, 56, 127, 131, 157
ACCESS public viewing gallery on the fourth floor

West Loop

Fujikawa, Johnson & Associates 1983, 1988

West Loop

Fujikawa, Johnson & Associates 1983, 1988

333 West Wacker Drive

Only ten years old and already an icon of the city, this is easily the most beautiful recent skyscraper in Chicago. Site sensitive, elegant and moving to look at from all angles this is an architectural *tour de force*. This dramatic 36-storey office tower is delightfully curved on one façade and angular on the other. The 365-foot-wide curve is a contextual response to the twisting of the Chicago River on which this façade fronts, and the rectilinear Loop front suits the triangular site perfectly.

Having swept up all possible awards and compliments this is one building it is impossible not to get excited about. The taut curve of the river-front façade is a reflective green glass curtain wall, reinforced by horizontal bullnoses at 6-foot intervals. The sheer green colour deepens and changes shade (sometimes seeming almost silvery) according to the river and the sun, always dramatically reflecting the urban landscape. This elevation has a calmness and meditative quality appropriate to an aquatic and urban setting. It is marvellous to stand, drive or sit on the El and watch the world curving by on this smooth surface as the location of 333 West Wacker makes it highly visible from many vistas. The top of the curve is set against a bevelled surface (chamfers), the slim flatness adding a tension to the fluid bend of the north façade as well as calling attention to the buildings crown. This curtain wall is supported by an elegant horizontally banded polychromatic granite base with highlights of black, grey and green marble or granite and brushed stainless steel.

The base houses mechanical facilities, cleverly disguised by the Art Deco stripes. Large medallions resembling ship portholes serve as ventilation louvres, a theme repeated in later KPF buildings. The steel bars of these round slatted windows are echoed in the Art Deco style railings along the serrated edge of the south-east façade. The downtown façade is geometrically set on the city grid, softened by the circular steps leading

Kohn Pedersen Fox 1983

Kohn Pedersen Fox 1983

up to the circular two-storey lobby. The materials of the exterior base are used in the green and silver lobby, continuing the lush ambience. There are many thoughtful touches such as the octagonal black columns that support the base echoing those found across the river at Merchandise Mart. The usual tower block amenities are found on the lobby level. Hidden below grade is a two-level parking garage.

ADDRESS 333 West Wacker Drive
ASSOCIATE ARCHITECTS Perkins & Will
CLIENT Urban Investment & Development Company
SIZE 800,000 square feet (74,000 square metres)
RTT Clark/Lake on Blue Line, Brown Line, Orange Line, Purple Line Express
BUS 16, 37, 41, 44, 61, 125
ACCESS public lobby

West Loop

Kohn Pedersen Fox 1983

Kohn Pedersen Fox 1983

225 West Wacker Drive

The 1980s' economic boom created such a wide market for speculative office buildings that a flood of out-of-town architects arrived on the scene in Chicago. Amongst the most successful of these has been the New York-based firm Kohn Pedersen Fox Associates. KPF have certainly made their mark on the city. Aside from 333 and 225 West Wacker, they have recently designed 900 North Michigan Avenue, Chicago Title & Trust and the 65-storey 311 South Wacker Drive, all very substantial schemes.

Completely different (apart from the repeated although modified port-hole motif), but in its own fashion as successful as its superlative neighbour, 333 West Wacker Drive, 225 is a rectilinear masonry box crowned by four aluminium spires. Within the base for these twinned spires is a barrel-vaulted roof and penthouse executive offices. Needless to say the lanterns are illuminated at night. This narrow tower is 31 storeys high and the straightforward exterior is a blend of granite and marble with an aluminium and insulated glass wall.

Set on a protracted, slender site, the building is bounded by West Wacker Drive, Franklin and Lake Streets, with entrance lobbies on both West Wacker Drive and Franklin Street. A riverfront arcade complements the dignified marble and granite clad vaulted lobby, planned, according to KPF's literature, as the building's formal front door and a transitional space between the exterior and interior of the building.

The stainless steel portal in the centre of the arcade is intended to pay reference to the metal construction of Chicago bridges. The two lobbies are decorated using the same sophisticated vocabulary and are connected by a vestibule. The Franklin Street atrium is 125 feet long and 35 feet wide and leads off into the requisite shops housed within the building. Behind the building and above the elevated train tracks is a six-storey parking garage.

West Loop

Kohn Pedersen Fox 1989

West Loop

Kohn Pedersen Fox 1989

While it is nowhere near as spectacular as 333, this is a well built and gracious structure that allows its illustrious predecessor to shine.

ADDRESS 225 West Wacker Drive
ASSOCIATE ARCHITECTS Perkins & Will
CLIENT The Palmer Group Limited
SIZE 710,000 square feet (66,000 square metres)
RTT Clark/Lake on Blue Line, Brown Line, Orange Line, Purple Line Express
BUS 16, 37, 41, 44, 61, 125
ACCESS public lobby

West Loop

Kohn Pedersen Fox 1989

Kohn Pedersen Fox 1989

West Loop

Morton International Building

Located on an asymmetrical delightfully urban plot along the west bank of the Chicago River, this edifice was built on an unusual 53,225-square-foot air-rights site. An extraordinary engineering design allows part of the building to partially hang over active railroad tracks. This south-west corner (55 x 150 feet encompassing twelve floors) is suspended by steel rolled section trusses which are cantilevered from the eastern part of the building. The exposed trusses have been likened to bridge elements seen on the Chicago River, adding a contextual element to this massive office block.

The two basic volumes forming the building, one a horizontal rectangle and the other a vertical rectangle, conspicuously reveal their programmatic functions. The shorter block houses a two-storey lobby, six-level parking lot and 250,000 square foot computer centre for use by Illinois Bell Telephone; the upright tower is obviously offices. A 30-foot-high covered promenade leads to the main entrance and a two story lobby. An arcade and an open air plaza overlook the river.

The exterior glass and aluminium curtain wall has been jazzed up with varying patterns of grey granite. Functional stipulations dictated the shade of grey (one of three) or its absence altogether in the intricately patterned façade. This visual stimulation somewhat alleviates the size and mass of these large rectilinear blocks.

ADDRESS 100 North Riverside Plaza
CLIENT Orix Real Estate Equities, Inc.
SIZE 1,100,000 square feet (102,000 square metres)
RTT Randoplh/Wells on Brown Line, Orange Line, Purple Line Express
BUS 20, 23, 56, 127, 131, 157
ACCESS public lobby and arcade

West Loop

Perkins & Will 1990

Perkins & Will 1990

Northwestern Atrium Center

A combined commuter terminal and 40-storey office complex, this building replaces the 1911 Beaux-Arts Chicago and Northwestern Train Station. Another glossy, glassy tower designed by Helmut Jahn, from a distance the cascading layers of blue-grey mirrored glass on the southern façade are quite beautiful, but the closer one gets the more the unfortunate shopping mall effect takes over. Designed originally as an addition for the Board of Trade, the scheme was shelved and later dusted off and adapted to its new site and function.

The reflective glass and steel walls are constructed as waves rhythmically repeating the same curves, inspired by a luxury train, 'The Twentieth Century Limited'. The overall tripartite configuration is accentuated by bands of dark blue enamelled aluminium running down the streamlined façade. Inside lighting fixtures, elevator details and coloured glass decorative elements continue the Art Deco motif. The two-level terminal, with its main entrance on Madison Street, is a series of atriums. The dramatic arched entranceway opens onto exposed structural steel criss-crossing the glazed roof. At ground level a 270-foot-long concourse incorporates 60,000 square feet of retail space. Escalators in the middle of this level lead to a third-floor elevator dock charmingly called a Skylobby, evocative of Jetsonian travel. The name is more exciting than the space.

An enclosed commuter bridge at the second floor of the atrium crosses Canal Street, providing access to Wacker Drive and the Central Loop.

ADDRESS 500 West Madison at North Canal Street
SIZE 1,600,000 square feet (150,000 square metres)
RTT Randolph/Wells on Brown Line, Orange Line, Purple Line Express
BUS 20, 23, 41, 56, 120, 122, 125, 127, 129, 130, 131, 157
ACCESS atriums accessible to public

West Loop

Murphy/Jahn 1987

West Loop

Murphy/Jahn 1987

T W Best Newsstand

This prototype newsstand was designed as a model environment capable of being adapted and reinterpreted in different settings.

A grey chequered floor and black modular units are offset by laminated architectural elements which serve a dual purpose as compositional ingredients and attention grabbers. The main focal point is a bright red frame cutting across the centre of the space, terminating in a delightful giant blue cone. This primary-coloured form is a witty peanut and potato-chip display. Yellow perforated metal banners hanging from the ceiling delineate the traffic flow. The colourful and efficient organisation make the items on sale easily accessible for the commuter rushing through.

Eva Maddox has designed another, later installation for T W Best at the Hotel Nikko (320 North Dearborn Street). This variation retains the progenitor's economical unit display although here entirely in wood and planned around a central counter. The Hotel Nikko branch has a calmer and more leisurely ambience suitable to its less trafficked surroundings.

Maddox is known for her extraordinary temporary installations, particularly at Merchandise Mart, the massive Art Deco showroom complex built in 1931 (designed by Graham, Anderson, Probst & White) and renovated from 1986 to 1991. Located between North Wells Street and North Orleans Street and normally only open to architects and designers, it is worth asking whether there are any current showrooms (they are very short-lived affairs) designed by Maddox.

ADDRESS Northwestern Terminal Building, 500 West Madison Street
INFORMATION ABOUT MERCHANDISE MART telephone 312-644 4664
RTT Randolph/Wells on Brown Line, Orange Line, Purple Line Express
BUS 20, 23, 41, 56, 120, 122, 125, 127, 129, 130, 131, 157
ACCESS open

West Loop

Eva Maddox Associates 1989

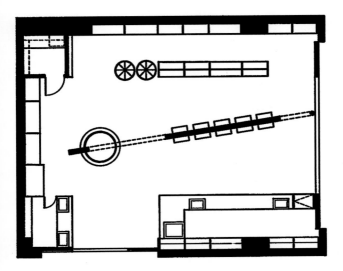

Eva Maddox Associates 1989

West Loop

Presidential Towers

Notable primarily for the financial mess the scheme has created, Presidential Towers has been a fiscal disaster since completion. Hoped to be the seed of a posh residential community in downtown Chicago capable of transforming a down-and-out neighbourhood into prime real estate, Presidential Towers has now become an icon of urban renewal failure. The developers, McHugh Levin in partnership with Dan Shannon Associates, received subsidies of one quarter of the overall cost from the federal government's Department of Housing and Urban Development. The City of Chicago also offered aid in the form of tax-exempt interim financing. This did not prevent the project from going into default.

Designed as a series of four identical 49-storey blocks, the towers have 2346 residential units linked at the base by an enclosed pedestrian mall. This covered walkway allows for 90,265 square feet of commercial space. These rather dull, light brown octagonal towers cut diagonally across two city blocks divided by a street. There are multilevel walkways connecting the complex over this street. Nothing about the exterior of the buildings identifies them as residential. It is their repetitive quality that makes these expensive apartment towers so visually unappealing. Only the luxurious amenities (health club, sun deck, rooftop track and basketball court) and expensive rent differentiate this design from welfare housing projects.

ADDRESS 555, 575, 605 and 625 West Madison Street (bordered by West Monroe, North Desplaines and North Clinton Streets)
STRUCTURAL ENGINEERS Chris P Stefanos Associates
COST $125 million
SIZE 2,000,000 square feet (186,000 square metres)
BUS 20, 23, 41, 56, 125, 131, 157
ACCESS public lobby and thoroughfare

West Loop

Solomon Cordwell Buenz & Associates 1986

Near West Side and South Loop

Peter Elliott Productions

Plunked directly opposite the rather dull Oprah Winfrey Harpo Studios (remodelled 1989, Nagle, Hartray & Associates) in this predominantly industrial neighbourhood is a gem of a building. A few blocks west of the Kennedy Expressway, it is a charming surprise to stumble across this classy façade of alternating smooth and rusticated precast renaissance stone, glass block and insulated glass. A solid rectilinear structure, it is topped by three metal bowed trusses supporting an elegant brushed aluminium canopy. The canopy is echoed in the reception area by an artful floating desk fabricated by a local sculptor.

The new facility is an expansion of one of the nation's leading tabletop commercial film director's studios. It includes a 70 x 70 foot central shooting space (with an enclosed tinted glass gallery walkway for observation of the ads being shot) with a high-tech temperature control system (in case the shoot involves ice-cream) and state-of-the-art electrical and mechanical systems. Sleek white, grey and the odd splash of red demarcate curved walls hiding a kitchen, client lounge and conference room. Terrazzo floors alternate with checker plate aluminium stairways; most of the trimmings are steel. The extra-large kitchen (allowing space for clients to observe preparations – when I visited hundreds of unwrapped chocolate bars were being prepped) is equipped with video monitors so shoots can be easily co-ordinated.

ADDRESS 1111 West Washington Boulevard
CLIENT Peter Elliott Productions
STRUCTURAL ENGINEERS Stearn-Joglekar, Limited
SIZE 10,000 square feet (930 square metres)
BUS 20, 23, 131
ACCESS none

Near West Side and South Loop

Hartshorne Plunkard, Limited 1993

Hartshorne Plunkard, Limited 1993

Greyhound Bus Terminal

A prototype facility for Greyhound Lines, part of an effort to revitalise their passenger terminals throughout the country, this building replaces a 35-year-old terminal in the Loop. Oddly relocated to a less central address, Greyhound and Trailways buses from all over the States now arrive at the new consolidated terminal.

A graceful architectonic structure, the depot is smaller than photographs suggest. Masonry clad, with alternating horizontal bands of brick and concrete, this two-level building is 35,000 square feet. Two canopies (suspended extensions of the roof) provide 10,000 square feet of sheltered space for 24 bus stalls. Refuelling and mechanical service facilities are housed underneath the canopies.

This programmatic requirement resulted in a structurally expressive roof that spans 45 feet. This technically sophisticated roof is supported by ten 50-foot dark blue steel masts connected to 3-inch-diameter steel rods and then stabilised with white cable crossbracing. Uplift caused by wind loads is controlled by additional steel tube compression members. Deliberately unfinished steel joists and perforated girders are visible on the underside of the covering. The second storey of the building has a serrated perimeter, designed to complement the visible crossbracing and limit solar heat gain.

ADDRESS 630 West Harrison Street at South Desplaines Street
STRUCTURAL ENGINEERS Cohen Barreto Marchertas, Inc.
COST $6.5 million
SIZE 58,400 square feet (5400 square metres) including bus canopies
RTT Clinton on Blue Line
BUS 60
ACCESS open

Near West Side and South Loop

Nagle, Hartray & Associates 1989

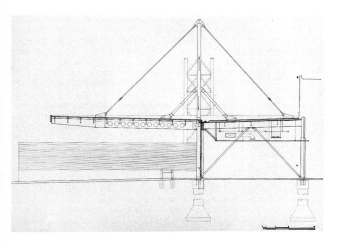

Nagle, Hartray & Associates 1989

Canal Center

This building, the Northern Trust Company Operations Center, was erected to house the bank's 'back office' operations. Relocated from several Loop locations, 2700 employees are now housed here on a 24-hour schedule. Although within a few blocks of the Chicago Union Station, the building is cut off from central downtown by the Chicago River and the Congress Expressway. The lack of local amenities resulted in a surprisingly suburban and self-sufficient building including a staff cafeteria, fitness centre, a car park, and daycare facilities.

Space in this non-high-rise building is equivalent to that in a 25-storey skyscraper. The long elevations and overall bulk have been mitigated with recesses at the Canal Street entry on the west and terracing on the east. Sandblasted grid work and a system of reveals wrap around the precast concrete perimeter, emphasising horizontality.

The formal lobby is quite dramatic, highlighted by a three-storey crystalline structural glass wall. The precast concrete skin traces an outline across this lobby window, weaving both sides of the building together. The main focal point of the lobby is a terraced glass block waterfall. The plan is organised around a central spine that serves as a 'main street' and connects all major areas on each level. Colour finishes and ceiling patterns change on each floor, serving as instant symbols of location and enlivening the otherwise identical 300-foot-long hallways.

ADDRESS 801 South Canal Street between Polk and Taylor Streets
CLIENT Northern Trust Company
SIZE 530,000 square feet (49,200 square metres)
RTT Clinton on Blue Line
BUS 37, 60
ACCESS none

Near West Side and South Loop

Eckenhoff Saunders Architects 1991

Eckenhoff Saunders Architects 1991

River City

Bertrand Goldberg, a seminal architect of late 20th century Chicago, is one of the last true idealists. The designer of the Marina City 'corncob' towers (1967), Goldberg continued his quest for the perfect urban agglomerate at River City. The motivation behind the endeavour is Goldberg's conviction that Chicago needs middle-income housing. The influx of middle-class residents propping up the tax base was an attempt to change downtown's demographics that did not win much government enthusiasm. All sorts of political obstructions followed the initial proposal in 1976 and it was not until Mayor Jane Byrne arrived on the scene in 1981 that planning permission and funding were allowed. Goldberg has written a great deal on the decline of our cities and his Utopian philosophy is, unfortunately, considered by many today to be antiquated. Fragmentation has become such a way of life that the idea of a self sufficient environment seems sadly alien and perverse. Goldberg states, 'As our cities shrink and atrophy, so does the life within them. If our cities are to remain a centre of civilisation they cannot serve as a 35 hour a week city inhabited by our poor. The original American vision of the city is one of synergy, growth and community'.

River City is a marvellous and poetic idea; sadly, construction details have not been treated as religiously as the concept and overall design. It is also a shame that the financial infrastructure was too weak to allow the project to be completed. Just Phase One (of a proposed five phases) is finished on the mile-long site directly on the bank of the south branch of the Chicago River. This is within walking distance of the financial district, the Sears Tower and other areas in the Loop. The overall megastructure consists of two parallell s-shaped residential blocks connected by a glazed atrium that rests on a rectilinear four-storey commercial base. Inspired by a mythical River Snake and Goldberg's

Bertrand Goldberg Associates, Inc. 1987

Bertrand Goldberg Associates, Inc. 1987

interpretation of chaos theory, the curvy cast-in-place concrete is simultaneously structural and sculptural. Computer research allowed the economic planning of cost-effective multiple use of internally fibre-glass lined standard steel formworks to cast the complex forms.

The stunning circular geometry was achieved by using a series of vertical concrete tubes spaced at intervals along the bending perimeter of two adjoining half-circles. Single columns have been placed at the halfway mark to support the floor slabs. As the tubes follow the S curve the form of the spaces between them varies, creating 22 varieties of apartments divided between 446 units. The glass-covered ten-storey atrium forms a kinetic internal street. Meandering between the two towers, intentionally evocative of a European street, with park benches, street lights and trees, it is an area designed for neighbours to meet. There is a park for residents on top of the jutting four-storey base. Amenities also include a grocery store, health centre, drugstore and parking facilities. One third of the existing plan is the 70-slip marina.

The exterior concrete façade, composed of juxtaposing curves and cantilevered balconies, has either rough-finish concrete or vertically fluted concrete fabricated by pinning glass-reinforced plastic strips to the custom-designed steel forms that the concrete was cast into.

ADDRESS 800 South Wells Street (at Polk Street)
STRUCTURAL ENGINEERS Bertrand Goldberg Associates, Inc.
COST $45 million approximately
SIZE 900,000 gross square feet (83,600 square metres)
RTT LaSalle on Blue Line, Brown Line, Orange Line, Purple Line Express
BUS 11, 22, 24, 36, 37
ACCESS public lobby and some commercial space

Bertrand Goldberg Associates, Inc. 1987

Bertrand Goldberg Associates, Inc. 1987

John G Shedd Oceanarium

The world's largest indoor marine mammal pavilion is an elegant, giant receptacle for an artificial Pacific Northwest outdoor environment.

The site, 1.8 acres of landfill on Lake Michigan, was already home to the Oceanarium's parent building, the 1929 neo-Classical Aquarium designed by Graham, Anderson, Probst & White. A shell-shaped extension at the rear of the old structure, the addition is respectful of the axis, scale and massing of the grand civic building. The aged white Georgia marble cladding from the existing back eastern wall was removed and it now covers the new structure, maintaining continuity of materials. Facing towards the lake, the Oceanarium's rear façade is a spectacular and enormous gently curved glass and steel curtain wall (an inch thick) that opens up the building, literally drawing Lake Michigan inside.

Divided into three levels, the centre of the facility is a 1000-seat steel-trussed column-free amphitheatre facing the main whale tank and the Lake (entering from quite a height, at the top the simulated harbour seems to amalgamate with the Lake). Hidden services, both mechanical and administrative offices, are cleverly placed beneath the theatre's tiered seating.

To the left of the central space are two restaurants and an orientation centre; to the right is a smaller auditorium. The dolphins, Beluga whales, seals, otters and other creatures can be observed both from above and under the water.

The entire interior simulates the coastal habitat, with painted concrete boulders, along 400 feet of twisting rugged nature trails with a jarrah wood path, passing 70 varieties of (real) trees and excellently executed papier-maché props.

Although controversial amongst animal-rights activists (a gang of protesters carry their banners reading 'Welcome to Whale Hell', etc. past

Lohan Associates 1991

the beautiful glass wall every time there is an hourly animal demonstration), the Oceanarium is a new breed of zoo infinitely more humane than the outdated facility it adjoins.

ADDRESS 1200 South Lake Shore Drive at Solidarity Drive
STRUCTURAL ENGINEERS Rittweger & Tokay
CLIENT The John G Shedd Aquarium
COST $43 million
SIZE 170,000 square feet (15,800 square metres)
BUS 6, 130, 146
ACCESS daily 09.00–17.00 March to October and 10.00–17.00
November to February; Thursday is free

Lohan Associates 1991

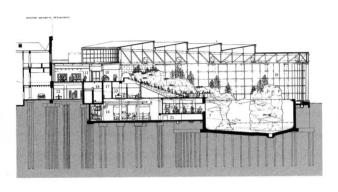

Lohan Associates 1991

Burnham Park Harbor Station

Redolent of Cape Cod or Long Island, this small maritime station conjures up mouthwatering thoughts of fresh lobster, clams and blueberry buckle. A white clapboard facility crested by a weather vane, this building could have been transplanted by a mysterious hurricane to Chicago from any site along the North Atlantic Coast. It makes a most pleasant and curious juxtaposition against the downtown post-urban skyline.

The straightforward, one-storey, bipartite L-shaped plan houses public restrooms, a food stand, public laundry and offices for the charter-boat director and a two-storey suite for the harbour master (with a super 360-degree view of the harbour). A gated breezeway separates the public amenities from those held for prearranged visitors. Built of unquestionably durable materials, the building is heavily insulated to withstand bad weather.

An adjacent sturdy shed provides an elegantly functional tabletop and water hoses for cleaning fish, very popular with the fishing public, particularly from May to October.

ADDRESS Burnham Park
CLIENT Chicago Park District
Marine Department
COST $628,898
SIZE Harbor Master Building,
1800 square feet (170 square metres);
Fish Cleaning Station,
200 square feet (19 square metres)
BUS 130, 146
ACCESS open to the public

Near West Side and South Loop

Bill Latoza/Chicago Park District 1990

Bill Latoza/Chicago Park District 1990

Pilsen

Cesar Chavez Elementary School

The Back of the Yards has traditionally been a port of entry neighbourhood. Adjacent to the former Chicago Union Stockyards, this heavily industrial area, bounded by railroad tracks and a canal, inspired Upton Sinclair's 1906 muckraking novel *The Jungle*. Originally the largest meat-packing base in America, the Back of the Yards' main industry has been decentralised since the advent of trucks and interstate highways. Today the area is still heavily populated by immigrants, currently Mexican-Americans.

In the midst of this urban fabric, on a small, shallow site (121 x 456 feet) sits the Cesar Chavez Elementary School. Wedged into this partial city block surrounded by the rear façades of commercial buildings, two-storey woodframe single-family residences and an empty lot, this is a school building that successfully addresses and attempts to engage the community.

The three-storey structure is divided into three separate masses. The library, gym and cafeteria blocks are extensions of the linear classroom/circulation spine. The entire structure is set back on the site, concealing the alley from view. Three separate playgrounds face the street, allowing visual supervision from surrounding houses. A children's palette of bright primary colours applied to masonry units and exterior steel components signals the school as a vibrant place of importance within the community.

The library – housed in a pyramid chosen, according to the architect Carol Ross Barney, for its 'visual impact as well as its non-colonial significance' – is lit at the apex at night, serving as a 'beacon in the neighbourhood'.

Once you enter the building, the hierarchy and three-tier separation of the primary, intermediate and upper grades is reinforced by the gradual loss of colour in the classrooms. This is a calculated attempt to represent

Ross Barney + Jankowski, Inc. 1993

Pilsen

Pilsen

Ross Barney + Jankowski, Inc. 1993

the activity of learning as one of increasing seriousness and a result of the students' own involvement. The classrooms are meant to be the students' personal canvas, no longer the domain of the architect.

ADDRESS 4747 South Marshfield Avenue
CLIENT Chicago Public Schools
STRUCTURAL ENGINEERS Martin/Lam, Inc.
CONTRACT VALUE $5.2 million
SIZE 64,000 square feet (6000 square metres)
TRANSPORT probably safest to drive or cab it
BUS 9, 47
ACCESS none

Pilsen

Ross Barney + Jankowski, Inc. 1993

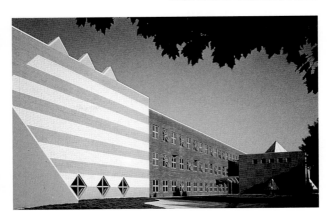

Pilsen

Ross Barney + Jankowski, Inc. 1993

Harrison Park Cultural and Recreational Center

Motivated by the Great Depression of the early 1930s, the conglomeration of Chicago's parks occurred when the federal government issued $6 million in bonds for WPA's expansion programmes. The Chicago Park District was incorporated in 1934 as the governing body of all parkland in Chicago.

The new building at Harrison Park is essentially a field house, a building type originating in 1888–1930 from the neighbourhood parks movement. As Chicago has such bitterly cold winters the field houses were designed as community clubhouses. Set in an existing park in a predominantly Mexican-American neighbourhood (the Mexican Fine Arts Museum is across the green), the centre serves a densely residential area. Designed as a crescent symbolically embracing the community, the new centre required new tree planting and landscaping. Rust-coloured concrete, green painted steel and copper columns in the entryway relax the fortress-like effect of very high windows (necessary for security). A gymnasium, boxing arena, music room, ping-pong room and art spaces adjacent to the already existing swimming pool are well used and appreciated by the locals.

ADDRESS 1824 South Wood Street at West 18th Place
CLIENT Community and Advisory Council of Harrison Park Chicago Park District, Department of Recreation
COST $3.39 million
SIZE 23,000 square feet (2100 square metres)
RTT 18th, Blue Line
BUS 9, 18, 50
ACCESS public

Julie Gross/Chicago Park District 1993

Pilsen

Pilsen

Julie Gross/Chicago Park District 1993

Near South Side and Bridgeport

McCormick Place North

An expansion of McCormick Place On-the-Lake, the new convention centre, a low-rise steel building, also accommodates a second exhibition hall allowing two major trade shows to occur simultaneously, doubling the size of the older facility. The two buildings are connected by an enclosed pedestrian tunnel and a bridge with fanciful cupolas that are visible from the highway. Designed around stacked halls, a result of the restrictive site, the exterior cable-suspended roof-truss system is spectacular to see, particularly when driving past. Constructed on air-rights, this allows the structure to hang over active commuter and freight railroad tracks.

This roof covers the main hall, measuring 480 x 780 feet. Cables are hung from twelve concrete pylons (inside, the pylons serve a double purpose and also contain the air-circulation systems) spaced in 120 x 240 foot bays, creating flexibility for different exhibitions. The pylons are joined to stiffener plates that then connect to tie-down pipes securing the roof to a podium. This podium, an elevated slab of 600 x 1350 feet, spans the working railways, supporting the main exhibition area and a warehouse space.

Clad with silver-grey aluminium panels attached to polished stainless steel mullions, the diagonal pattern of the roof trusses is repeated on the façade by patterning on the glass band of windows at the top.

ADDRESS 450 East 23rd Street
COST $170 million
SIZE 1,500,000 square feet (140,000 square metres)
BUS 3, 4, 21, 127
ACCESS varies from show to show

Near South Side and Bridgeport

Skidmore, Owings & Merrill, Inc. 1986

Skidmore, Owings & Merrill, Inc. 1986

Chinatown Square

The first, commercial phase of an ambitious scheme, 7.8 acres of the 32-acre project have been completed. Roughly $3.5 million was spent on infrastructure. The site was once the yards of the Sante Fe Railroad and required an extensive clean-up. Traces of creosote and benzene by-products meant a clay barrier had to be laid down and planting of edible vegetation has been restricted. Chinatown has needed to expand for quite a long time. Across the street from the old railroad yards, the new site is a natural area to spread onto. The outside perimeter is the Chicago River, and a bridge or link to the other side is hoped for in the far future. McCormick Place, the expo complex, is also expected to become part of the community, attracting conventioneers. A quarter (approximately 20,000) of Chicago's Chinese American population live in Chinatown: the new scheme hopes to provide housing for 2000. There is a master plan spanning the next decade accommodating the construction of townhouses, apartments, a Chinese television station, an Oriental Garden, a community center and a trade centre.

The new complex has red and green pagoda-style elevators and stair towers, bilingual street signs, diamond shaped windows, and ornamental seals periodically inserted into the brickwork to continue the dialect of the existing bordering Chinatown.

ADDRESS Archer Avenue, Cermak Road, Chicago River, 18th Street and Wentworth Avenue
STRUCTURAL ENGINEERS Seymour Lepp & Associates
SIZE 200,000 square feet (18,600 square metres)
RTT Cermak/Chinatown on Red Line
BUS 21, 42, 62, 62 Express
ACCESS open

Harry Weese & Associates 1993

Harry Weese & Associates 1993

Comiskey Park

In 1908 Charles Comiskey purchased 15 acres of land that had supposedly been used for athletic activities since the 1860s and had a ballpark built on the property for the Chicago White Sox. This Major League stadium, the oldest in the nation, was designed by Zachary Taylor Davis.

Eighty years later, when the White Sox were contemplating relocating to St Petersburg, Florida, the Illinois State Assembly and the current Mayor, James R Thompson, created legislation for a public-private partnership to fund the construction of a new stadium to keep the team in Chicago. A reciprocal financial arrangement was reached, funding for construction being generated by a 2 per cent hotel/motel tax in Chicago and the government getting a percentage of the White Sox's revenue. This earns Chicago and the State of Illinois around $180 million annually.

The new Comiskey Park is directly opposite the 1910 original, which was deemed too costly to rehabilitate and was therefore torn down and replaced by a parking lot. All that remains of the original is home plate.

The first stadium devoted solely to baseball to be built in the USA since 1972, Comiskey Park is a both an economic feat and a step backward for urban planning. Completely oblivious to the city life surrounding it, this project was conceptualised in shopping-mall mode. Admittedly the site is in a rough neighbourhood. It is across the Dan Ryan Expressway from the Robert Taylor Homes and a few blocks east of Stateway Gardens, two of the city's most rundown, crime-ridden, gang-infested housing projects. Yet this is no excuse for the scheme's complete lack of engagement with its environment. The building is stranded in an ocean of 7000 parking spaces and the exterior pedestrian circulation ramps look like barricades against an invasion. All programmatic functions, such as food stalls or souvenir shops, are internalised, exacerbating the lonely fortress effect. No reference to the relevant historical importance of the

Hellmuth, Obata & Kassabaum, Inc. 1991

Hellmuth, Obata & Kassabaum, Inc. 1991

site is evident, a real shame, as it would have been so appropriate to incorporate a fragment of the old stadium into the new.

Philip Bess, a Chicago architect who proposed an alternative, more urbane scheme, has been an outspoken critic of the New Comiskey: 'In terms of ballpark and urban aesthetics, the outstanding and overwhelming fact about the new Comiskey Park (and its adjacent surface parking lots) is the way it requires the city of Chicago to do all the adjusting; it is essentially anti-urban and does not accommodate city life'.

Although the architects hoped that the beige concrete panels and the series of arched windows would be reminiscent of the original building, the blue spandrels, green mullions, tinted glass and unfortunate street furniture dotting the parking lots, speak a bland suburban language.

All this aside, the stadium is comfortable, well-functioning and has no obstructed-view seats. The upper decks are at quite an angle, a 35-degree slope, but there are most definitely no pillars anywhere in the 160 feet between the viewer and the field! Commendably, there is seating for 400 handicapped spectators and access to all levels. Forty ticket windows are available, eight escalators, a Sony Jumbotron exploding scoreboard and, most importantly, an increased number of restrooms for women – three to each men's room.

ADDRESS West 35th Street and South Shields Avenue
STRUCTURAL ENGINEERS Thornton-Tomasetti, Inc.
COST $135.47 million
SIZE 990,000 square feet (92,000 square metres)
RTT Sox/35th on Red Line
BUS 24, 35, 39
ACCESS check game schedule

Hellmuth, Obata & Kassabaum, Inc. 1991

Near South Side and Bridgeport

Hellmuth, Obata & Kassabaum, Inc. 1991

Hyde Park

John Crerar Library

Inaugurated in 1892, the University of Chicago's Neo-Gothic master plan was designed by Henry Ives Cobb. Academic buildings congregated around the ancient collegiate quadrangle were built to medieval proportions and decorated with gargoyles, corbels, and lancet windows. When in 1978 the University decided to consolidate its science and medicine reference collection with that of the John Crerar Library they published stringent guidelines. Neo-Gothic influence had to be acknowledged while fitting in with more recent eclectic additions on the site.

The new library completes the eighth quadrangle on campus. Four storeys high, 300 feet long and 100 feet wide, the reinforced concrete structure is finished in buff Indiana limestone. A few Gothic references are apparent: the choice of materials, fenestrations, and the freestanding arch calling attention to the off-centre main entrance. The windows diminish in size with each level; a glazed curtain wall on the first floor, a sunscreen cantilevered over the smaller second floor openings and on the top level the windows have become slits.

ADDRESS 5730 South Ellis Avenue at East 57th Street
ASSOCIATE ARCHITECTS Loebl, Schlossman & Hackl
STRUCTURAL ENGINEERS LeMessurier Consultants, Inc.
COST approx. $13 million
SIZE 60,000 square feet (14,900 square metres)
RTT for safety reasons it is not advisable to take the L in this area; it is also not a good idea to walk in the surrounding areas off the campus
BUS 4, 6, 55
METRA ELECTRIC 55th/56th/57th Street Station
ROAD Lake Shore Drive south exit at 51st, 53rd, 57th Street
ACCESS Monday–Saturday 09.00–17.00

Hyde Park

Hugh Stubbins Associates 1985

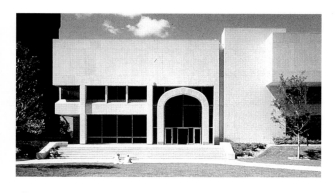

Hugh Stubbins Associates 1985

Kersten Physics Teaching Center

The strongest lasting impression of this narrow, three-storey science facility is its clever circulation system. Designed around a gabled corridor forming an energetic entrance atrium, it continues as a long, narrow hanging spine that becomes the fundamental meeting place within the building. Controlling the waterfall of stairs leading to various levels, this backbone terminates (on the second level) as a pedestrian bridge across 57th Street connecting to the Research Institute. On the third floor the corridor ends as a gridded wall looking onto the student lounge. Organised around this central backbone are the offices, 13 laboratories, lecture halls and classrooms that comprise the buildings programme. A lecture hall is on the ground floor and there is a rooftop observatory.

The entire hallway is attached to a completely glazed exterior wall and topped by a triangular running skylight exaggerating the verticality of the building while simultaneously opening it up to the quadrangle it completes. This south-west wall is adjacent to the main west elevation, a series of glass-walled setbacks forming three levels of open sky terraces and an outdoor scientific gallery. For a serious scientific centre it is pleasantly accessible. In keeping with the neo-Gothic campus, the street façade is formal Indiana limestone with proportions and scale reflecting the surrounding structures.

ADDRESS 5720 South Ellis Avenue
ASSOCIATE ARCHITECT Harold H Hellman/University Architect
COST $6 million
SIZE 57,200 square feet (5300 square metres)
BUS 4, 6, 55, 59
ROAD Lake Shore Drive, south exit at 57th Street
ACCESS open

Hyde Park

Holabird & Root 1985

Hyde Park

Holabird & Root 1985

Suburbs South-West

Glendale Heights Post Office

Visibility from the highway was a primary concern in the design of this suburban post office. The only retail operation in an industrial park, the architects planned the façade so it would be readable while cruising past in an automobile. Red, white, and blue, this patriotic building intentionally resembles the Stars & Stripes.

Amongst all this brilliant colour, red and buff brick is still discernible, an attempt at relating to the language of the surrounding utilitarian warehouses. Three-quarters of the front façade is royal blue glazed brick stuck below a horizontal tier of red and white striped wall with angular undulations (the wall pointedly folds in and out). This has the desired effect of making the building resemble a flag billowing in the wind. The two-tone striations wrap all the way around the large shed structure. Golden triangular skylights sit on the roof and are then repeated as foils for the roof drainage system. The blue façade is sprinkled with a symmetrical series of small square windows, allowing daylight in but cleverly preventing a view out to the unpicturesque front parking lot. This bright cheery façade embodies the user-friendly ambience prevalent throughout the scheme.

The simple plan consists of two programmatic parts: a large workroom-warehouse for sorting and processing mail, and a smaller customer area inserted into the front of the warehouse. There are two adjacent main entrances, one directly to the private mailboxes and another to the service counter. Using economical and hard-wearing materials, the dynamic interior continues the flag motif. A larger-than-life Postal Eagle flies across the industrial vinyl mat in the vestibule. Wide waves of colour spotted with stars ripple along the linoleum floor. Even the florescent fixtures are arranged in a funky, flag-waving fashion as stars in a blue background, and in the private mailbox area as white strip lighting against a red ceiling

Ross Barney & Jankowski, Inc. 1989

meant to symbolise stripes. The lockboxes are unusually arranged in three individual islands, across from the red granite waist-high tabletops used for last-minute envelope addressing. Although the imagery is obvious it works so well because it has been executed in a delightful, jovial manner.

There are many conceptual and stylistic similarities between this public facility and the elementary school recently completed by Ross Barney & Jankowski (Cesar Chavez Elementary School, see page 232). For instance: the recognisable programmatic use of colour combined with ordinary materials such as brick and steel, the use of Le Corbusier-inspired 'windows to the heavens', and the creation of architectonic spaces with angular shapes and overlapping planes.

It is wonderful that civic buildings can be made so amiable and energetic. Going to the post office need not be a dull, sterile experience!

ADDRESS Brandon Drive at Bloomingdale Road
STRUCTURAL ENGINEERS Martin/Martin, Inc.
CLIENT United States Postal Service
SIZE 24,000 square feet (2200 square metres)
COST $2 million
ROAD 290 Expressway west, take a right turn to western suburbs, exit Route 64 west to Bloomingdale Road; after approximately 9 miles turn left onto Brandon Drive
ACCESS public

Suburbs South-West

Ross Barney & Jankowski, Inc. 1989

Ross Barney & Jankowski, Inc. 1989

Oakbrook Terrace Tower

An urban phenomenon has been transplanted into suburbia. The tallest building in the suburbs, visible from every approach, this skyscraper is located at a major highway intersection, 25 miles west of the city. Thirty-one storeys and 418 feet high, it towers over the neighbouring commercial and residential buildings. Since the 1970s businesses have been migrating to the city's outskirts at a rapidly increasing pace, usually taking the shape of low industrial parks or sprawling campuses. Exurbia is now the nation's largest area of construction and growth. The addition of underground parking facilities at the Oakbrook Terrace Tower is an indication of the rising land values in this region.

The architects have succeeded in their aim: to construct a singular object with a distinct skyline identity. A blue-green and grey glass-faced octagon, the tower is beautifully detailed. Unusually understated for Helmut Jahn, this edifice is not too shiny or glossy. Fret glass spandrels set in an orthogonal grid are patterned with small dots against a grey background, giving the appearance of a metal mesh. An inverted v is the decorative motif, appearing at several different scales. The roof is pointed and the main entrance echoes this configuration. The form was generated by the play of the vertical and horizontal patterns joining with the building's four diagonal facesg. The ceremonial v is engraved in white marble in the five-storey lobby and the motif recurs throughout the interior.

ADDRESS 1 Tower Lane
STRUCTURAL ENGINEERS Cohen Barreto Marchertas, Inc.
SIZE 714,000 square feet (66,300 square metres)
ROAD 290 west to Roosevelt Road, west to 83; south to first stop light; right on Spring Road to Tower Lane
ACCESS public lobby

Murphy/Jahn 1986

Murphy/Jahn 1986

McDonald's Corporation Lodge and Training Center

Nicknamed Hamburger University, this was built as an exemplary corporate training campus. Two large low buildings are placed in an 81 acre site. The Training Center and Lodge are constructed with friendly materials – wood, brick and Wisconsin lannin stone – in a recognisable Prairie School pot-pourri mingling Frank Lloyd Wright with hints of Mies van der Rohe in the meticulous detailing. The Training Center is organised around clusters of classrooms and offices circling a two-storey, skylit atrium, the centrepiece of a large galleria (decorated with wonderful McDonald's memorabilia) designed to encourage socialising and ideas exchange. An auditorium, seminar/conference rooms, and laboratories are available. The 3000 students who pass through annually live in the 154-room Lodge, planned with the Hyatt Corporation who run the facility. Relaxingly luxurious (with a definite institutional undertone), the Lodge contains both recreational and relaxational spaces designed to continue the social and edifying goals of the training week.

The Lodge has been designed around a 150-year-old Ohio Buckeye tree. The oak forest setting includes a McNature Trail. A partially covered concrete bridge connects the two buildings, affording a windy path over Lake Fred, where fake ducks bob up and down on the calming waters.

ADDRESS 2715 Jorie Boulevard, Oak Brook
SIZE 330,000 square feet (30,660 square metres)
STRUCTURAL ENGINEERS Chris P Stefanos Associates
ROAD 290 west, to 188 west, exit at Route 83 south, turn right on 31st Street, turn left (east) on Jorie Boulevard
ACCESS none

Suburbs South-West

Lohan Associates 1984, 1990

Suburbs South-West

Lohan Associates 1984, 1990

Speigel Corporate Headquarters

This prepossessing building stands at the intersection of two major highways accessible directly off an exit ramp. Headquarters of catalogue-merchandising company Speigal, a dichotomous exterior powerfully expresses the disparate aspects of the site horizontally, one side being adjacent to the freeway and the rear looking out over the Hidden Lake Forest Preserve.

The road façade is a formal rectilinear grid alternating bands of precast concrete and light grey granite panels with an aluminium and green glass curtain wall, exposing every other level of the structural steel system. It is topped by a microwave communications tower adding height (visible from a speeding car) to the 14-storey building.

The other side of the building, attached by a narrow sandwich filling layer, undulates and gently curves in homage to the informal forms found in nature. Hanging over a man-made retention pond, this beautiful serpentine curtain wall has the same green-tinted glass alternating with bands of ceramic-coated glass spandrels. A low circular building jutting out over the pond houses a two-storey cafeteria. This space-age projection allows employees to be surrounded by nature, avoiding the usual suburban sea of cars.

ADDRESS 3500 Lacey Road, Downers Grove
CLIENT Hamilton Partners, Inc.
COST $59 million
SIZE 660,000 square feet (61,000 square metres)
ROAD 290 West to I-88 West, North on 355 to Butterfield Road, exit West to Wood Creek Drive
ACCESS none

Skidmore, Owings & Merrill, Inc. 1992

Skidmore, Owings & Merrill, Inc. 1992

Illinois State Toll Highway Authority

On a grassy meadow smack next door to the highway, the new midrise ISTHA building overlooks its main concern. But the building faces away from the tollway to its west which is invisible from the interior, and as it is organised around an internal central courtyard it seems to be ignoring the roadway as well. According to the architects the façade is covered with images evocative of cars. Not very convincing, curved precast concrete columns decorated with circular blobs of concrete (tollbooth coins perhaps) look vaguely like automobile bumpers and the blue/green tinted fenestrations are farfetched resemblances of headlight fixtures.

The interior, infinitely more interesting than the exterior, is divided by a cylindrical atrium wedged in between two parallel rectangular structures that meet at the ends in service cores. The fracture is the entrance leading into a two-storey atrium with a floating terrazo staircase visible straight ahead. Mechanical references are more apparent here with exposed steel soffits supporting the ribbed skylights and interior columns resembling engine parts. Industrial-style walkway bridges connect private conference spaces and allow views of the greenery flourishing on the ground floor.

Mostly occupied by administrative offices, the facility also has a secret area where the tolls from across Northern Illinois are counted.

ADDRESS 1 Authority Drive, Downers Grove
STRUCTURAL ENGINEERS Martin/Martin
CLIENT Illinois State Toll Highway Authority
COST $25.5 million
SIZE 185,000 square feet (17,000 square metres)
ROAD take 290 west towards 88, west to 355 south, exit Ogden Avenue
ACCESS none

Suburbs South-West

Lohan Associates 1991

Lohan Associates 1991

Frederick T Owens Village Center

Opposite a sprawling shopping mall that is (scarily enough) the actual hub of the town, three buildings orthogonally ring a man-made retention lake. The complex includes a village hall with government offices and classrooms, a civic meeting centre with gallery space as well as a banqueting hall, a recreation building and an outdoor amphitheatre that projects over the lake. A theatre is planned to complete the quartet. To create visual coherence internal functions have been visibly expressed by external form: circular pavilions indicate meeting halls and columned galleries stand for lobbies.

The spire-topped clock tower of the three-storey symmetrical village hall is the centrepiece of the complex, intended as a new point of reference for the village. A semi-covered curving walkway over the water connects the buildings.

ADDRESS 14700 South Ravinia Avenue, Orland Park
CLIENT Village of Orland Park
SIZE 87,400 square feet (8100 square metres)
COST $11.5 million
ROAD take I-55, exit LaGrange Road south, right on 145th, left on Ravinia
ACCESS public

Perkins & Will 1989

Perkins & Will 1989

Suburbs North

Ameritech Center

Grandiose in scale and formal in style, Ameritech has created its own self-sufficient universe, a small internal city, in the middle of suburban Hoffman Estates. This entirely non-smoking environment houses 2500 employees. Aside from offices, conference space, and a library, the facilities include a sports club, wellness centre and an eating emporium. In the lower depths of the building there is a secret laboratory that simulates and creates new communications systems.

The basic symmetrical plan of the building consists of two crosses joined by a central spine. The main artery off the drive actually cuts right underneath the middle of the building and leads directly to parking. The entry to the immense, grandiose lobby is on the second floor, although it feels like ground level. Security throughout the building is reminiscent of that at an international airport.

Once allowed past the vast glass doors at the back of the lobby, you have arrived at Main Street, the organisational element of the building which functions much like a typical high street. Two identical four-storey atriums in each wing are connected by a tiered network of suspended high-tech walkways that traverse the entire building, cutting directly through workspaces. It is incredibly disorienting. Take a map, experienced tour guide, and hiking boots.

ADDRESS 2000 West Ameritech Center Drive, Hoffman Estates
STRUCTURAL ENGINEERS Chris P Stefanos Associates
SIZE 1,300,000 square feet (121,000 square metres)
COST $304 million
ROAD I-90 west, north on Roselle Road, left on Central: Ameritech is off Central
ACCESS none

Lohan Associates 1991

Lohan Associates 1991

Sears Merchandise Group Headquarters

Significant as a social phenomenon, this is the relocation site for 6000 employees who used to occupy offices in the 1450-foot-tall Sears Tower. Now they occupy a suburban campus consisting of low-rise buildings. Motivated not only by financial incentives, apparently the skyscraper premises were destructive of corporate culture and found alienating by the people working there. The company chose to join McDonalds, Kraft, Spiegal, Motorola and many others in moving to the 'burbs.

A typical, uniformly blue-glass-clad complex, this is a rather nondescript set-up. Well designed and well built, several four- to six-storey buildings are connected by a central atrium originally called 'Main Street'. The banal design houses the average number of facilities in an attempt to be the usual all-inclusive environment.

For many reasons (tourists passing through, sheer size and impersonality) one can understand that the Sears Tower was a difficult place to work, but how can the anonymity and the lack of neighbourhood, specialness and surrounding amenities in this typical homogenous little world be the solution?

ADDRESS Higgins Road, Hoffman Estates
CLIENT Sears Roebuck & Company
STRUCTURAL ENGINEERS Cohen Barreto Marchertas, Inc.
SIZE 1,900,000 square feet (176,500 square metres)
ROAD I-90/94 north-west, I-90 to Hoffman Estates; exit Route 90 north to Route 72 and turn left onto Higgins Road
ACCESS none

Suburbs North

Perkins & Will 1992

Perkins & Will 1992

Cooper Lighting Showroom

Remarkable for its architecturally interesting contents rather than the structure itself, this is an extraordinary product showroom. An information and education centre organised as an interactive museum with hands-on experiments, the facility, known professionally as The Source, has accommodated over 14,000 visitors since opening.

A dramatic glass and steel staircase leads to the introductory room filled with glass lit displays and TV screens. Demonstrations of all major light sources are given in the fundamentals room, a circular space filled with the most intriguing props. A series of well-designed spaces follows, each devoted to a particular aspect of lighting, organised around three principles: technology, effect and performance. A row of example settings, residential, commercial and office, are divided by partitions yet connected by a linear series of columns and are used to demonstrate varying lighting solutions, for example, how warmer coloured light creates a friendlier atmosphere.

After this each space is devoted to one particular type of product in all its possible forms. The power of repetition and conglomeration is apparent in the sheer fascination of seeing all these fixtures in one place. In the overhead lighting room the ceiling resembles a piece of Swiss cheese, allowing designers not only to study effects but to compare mountings.

The cohesive design of the programme/spaces brings home the spatial power of lighting in a logical straightforward fashion.

ADDRESS 400 Busse Road, Elk Grove Village
SIZE 20,000 square feet (1900 square metres)
ROAD 290 to 83 north, exit at Oakton, turn left onto Busse Road
ACCESS by appointment

Booth Hansen & Associates 1991

Booth Hansen & Associates 1991

American Academy of Pediatrics Headquarters

Dignified and serious, this hybrid combination of classical and vaguely postmodern imagery surrounded by fields and a landscaped lawn creates a peaceful, sedate vista. Visible from the highway, particularly when illuminated at night, the structure stands out from its unattractive neighbours. Structurally a steel frame clad with a two-tone skin of banded brick and limestone, it is refreshing to see a contemporary corporate building in the suburbs without a predominantly glass façade.

The entranceway is at mid level, cutting through the sloping site, leading axially through the lobby and ending in the large atrium that overlooks a man-made lake.

A large conference room faces the lake on the ground level; offices and meeting rooms occupy the other two levels. Wood, terrazo floors and muted primary shades continue throughout the calm interior. Plants abound both inside and outside in the landscaped gardens.

Two fabulous skylights break through the roof over the entrance lobby and the atrium, adding to the dramatic night image.

Suburbs North

ADDRESS 141 Northwest Point Boulevard, Elk Grove Village
ROAD Kennedy Expressway to I-90 to Elmhurst Road to Oakden to 83/ Busse Road, right onto Handmeyer leads into Arlington Heights Road
ACCESS none

Hammond, Beeby & Babka 1990

Hammond, Beeby & Babka 1990

Bradford Exchange

A scheme done in three stages, the final phase being designed by Thomas Hickey & Associates. Rich with avant-garde ideas and hilarious in their hodge podge, bizarre execution, this building (housed in a renovated warehouse and an adjacent ex-Chrysler dealership) is like a project by a wild architectural student gone mad. The building's completely mismatched façades clash shamelessly on this suburban commercial strip. Exterior walls (with differing heights) alternate between glass and mirror with asymmetrical patterns and a near-naked trellised rear wall.

The interior is a fantasy of misguided exotic ideas made all the more eccentric by the building's programme. The headquarters of the world's largest traders of collector plates, there is actually a small trading floor where you can follow the prices of Rockwell's Golden Moments or the ever-popular Scarlett O'Hara plates. A half disassembled museum next to the trading floor used to be so popular collectors were bussed in.

From the main entrance it is possible to glimpse the weirdness ahead. Three types of gardens unfold through the length of the building. Each one has a theme; either bamboo or orchids surround the wooden path bisecting the waterway that runs the length of the office space. Funky, suspended frosted glass and cable bridges swing precariously above the miniature forest. Above these bridges is the most extraordinary addition, silicone-coated glass-fibre tensile structures that overlap and are held up by tent poles and cables, concealing the industrial ceiling of the building.

ADDRESS 9333 North Milwaukee Avenue, Niles
STRUCTURAL ENGINEERS Getty, White, and Mason
SIZE 175,000 square feet (16,000 square metres)
ROAD Kennedy to Edens North to Dempster West to Milwaukee Avenue
ACCESS none

Weese Hickey Weese 1992

Weese Hickey Weese 1992

Municipal Fueling Facility

An 8-foot-high brick wall links all the programme fundamentals for this Public Works service centre. Enclosing the entire 1 acre corner site, the wall works its way around the perimeter, adapting to the various functional, aesthetic, and landscaping requirements. Alternating between serving as a building wall, a lower screen wall and a support system for the cantilevered secondary roof, the structure even curves to accommodate an oak before mutating into a circular bathroom/storage building.

The middle stage of a three-phase civic project, the gas station is placed at the end of the entire scheme. The top end consists of a building housing administrative offices and a truck repair garage completed in 1984; to date the middle is unfinished.

Basically a freestanding brick and concrete structure, the pumping island is covered by an elongated elliptical steel canopy that appears to float but is supported by six sets of paired narrow steel columns. The smaller, rectilinear cover below it points towards the bathroom/storage space, providing a covered walkway to the corner cylinder. The pedestrian canopy rests on three steel supports and a glass brick wall. The glass blocks are repeated as a circular ribbon around the corner bathroom/storage space and are illuminated at night.

ADDRESS 1333 Shermer Avenue, Glenview
STRUCTURAL ENGINEERS Don Belford Associates
COST $1 million
ROAD I-94 north to Lake Avenue; west over bridge, 4 miles, at intersection of Shermer and Lake turn right
METRA ELECTRIC Milwaukee District North Line train to Glenview; bus 210 WB to Shermer
ACCESS none

Lubotsky Metter Worthington & Law 1988

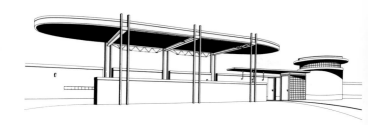

Lubotsky Metter Worthington & Law 1988

House in Wilmette

Wilmette is one of the older, more established residential communities in Greater Chicago, boasting large, solid homes built mainly between the latter half of the 1880s and 1930s. On this quiet, pretty residential street sits the perfect colonial two-kids-and-a-dog home. This delicate small house is traditional suburbia at its best. Modern in its simplicity but historical in its vocabulary, the plain façade and elegant porch are contextually sensitive, blending in perfectly with the surrounding larger homes. Set at the front edge of the site, the grey stucco structure is encircled by a wide wooden porch with fragile columns supporting an entablature. These columns wane significantly towards the top, visually lengthening the height of the porch. The reinvented typical white porch railing has spindles, three-quarters of an inch square, enhancing the dainty effect without seeming too precious.

The interior is organised vertically owing to the restrictive plot size (50 x 170 feet). Three storeys high, it contains two bedrooms, two bathrooms, a sunroom and a dining room that continue with the same vocabulary and materials as the exterior. Great effort was put into good craftsmanship and the interior includes lots of hand-crafted wood detailing.

The only thing missing from this cinematic dream house is the white picket fence.

ADDRESS 821 Forest Avenue, Wilmette
SIZE 2600 square feet (240 square metres)
STRUCTURAL ENGINEERS Gullaksen Getty & White
ROAD I-94 to 41, exit at Wilmette Avenue to Forest Avenue
ACCESS none

Hammond, Beeby & Babka 1986

Hammond, Beeby & Babka 1986

Private Residence

Treating each function as a separate entity, the plan for this one-bedroom house with guest rooms, swimming pool and cabana resembles that of a village. Originating from a request of the clients that the house be based around an elongated egg, each room has become a spatial entity in its own right, rotating off each other and the original ellipse. Each room becomes a separate volume, with individual colour, form, materials and rooftop. Symbolically and literally, the trace of the original ellipse goes through the house, leaving an imprint through rug, wood floor and tile.

Two decaying obelisks mark the paved plaza entranceway. According to Tigerman, these symbolise the evacuation of the eternal sought-after original space, a metaphysical Garden of Eden. The square cloakroom, cylindrical library, and telephone kiosk are all placed on the internal brick street as separate components. Kitchen, dining space, living room, media room and bedrooms are self-contained spaces on the outskirts of the settlement. The round dining area with signature Tigerman columns and a wonderful high ceiling lends grandeur to the scheme. There is an intriguing, playful juxtaposition of angles and curves as one moves through the house.

This multilayered project follows an intellectual process of testing of what Tigerman describes as 'the potential of activation in architecture as a vehicle to overcome the stasis common to building'.

ADDRESS 1940 Park West Avenue, Highland Park
STRUCTURAL ENGINEERS Beer Gorski & Graff
SIZE 6500 square feet (600 square metres)
ROAD I-94 to 41, exit on Central Avenue, turn left onto St John's Avenue, right onto Park West Avenue
ACCESS none

Tigerman McCurry 1988–1990

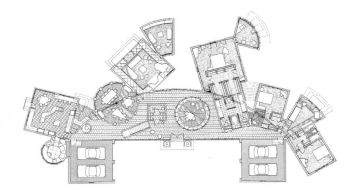

Tigerman McCurry 1988–1990

North Shore Congregation Israel Synagogue Addition

In 1964 a spectacular synagogue designed by Minoru Yamasaki, a vast white free-flowing concrete structure obviously inspired by nature, was erected on this bluff facing Lake Michigan. An unusual interior structural system supports a quirky, petal-like roof that is very 1960s; from the outside one imagines luxurious beanbag pews inside. Seating 1100 congregants (in a rather formal fashion – not beanbags at all), the sanctuary proved too vast for everyday intimate services. Hence the addition, completed in 1984, designed with a very different vocabulary.

With an historicist masonry (sandstone-coloured brick) façade in a cylindrical form with a simplified Palladian portico stuck on, the new building is the complete antithesis of Yamasaki's modern structure. This diversity adds richness, as an attempt at repeating or copying such an idiosyncratic building would have been disastrous.

Based on the layering of space, the new, much smaller (300 seats) addition is a 40-foot-square cube placed within a series of outer circles. Visually symbolic, much of the design process involved the participation of the Rabbi, allowing the incorporation of traditional meaning into the layout. Judaic symbols such as the Star of David formed the basis for details such as the large chandelier in the sanctuary. Disparate religious and social functions are expressed with different forms: the sanctuary is circular and the social hall is a rectangle which contains a noteworthy, lovely series of colourful paintings by the Israeli artist Heinz Seelig.

The modulation of light was an important issue, and the outer circulation ring is punctuated by both large circular windows quite low down and small square cut-outs around the outer rim. A 6-foot circular skylight in the sanctuary allows natural light to pour in over the elegant oak space

Hammond, Beeby & Babka 1984

Hammond, Beeby & Babka 1984

inspired by the vernacular synagogues of Eastern Europe. A perfunctory balcony overlooking the sanctuary calls to mind traditional Orthodox synagogues. The blend of Ashkenazi and Sephardic influences (the two major geographical branches of Judaism) lend a diversity expressive of the architects' desire to show the heterogeneity of the Jewish community in North America. An eminently suitable building.

ADDRESS 1185 Sheridan Road, Glencoe
ROAD Kennedy north, turn right onto Lake Hook Road, which turns into Sheridan Road
ACCESS call before you go

Hammond, Beeby & Babka 1984

Hammond, Beeby & Babka 1984

Private Family Residence

Situated on a scenic 3 acre plot, a wooded ravine overlooking Lake Michigan, is this dramatic, luxurious home. The clients had specific requirements: their preference was for Modernism, the house had to have large entertaining spaces affording views of the Lake and be a showcase for their spectacular contemporary art collection. The clients interviewed around 20 architects before deciding on Arquitectonica.

The structure is a sprawling one-storey zigzag placed at the top of the site with three lake fronts. A paved courtyard is partially enclosed by the garage wing creating a private enclave in this residential neighbourhood. Clad in a mosaic of mostly pink granite that has been randomly flamed and honed, with a black base and a bluestone terrace, the exterior is an irregular meeting of various angles and planes. The stacked roof is tilted and raised and culminates by cantilevering out past the master bedroom. Assymetrically geometrical windows have been arbitrarily placed, either framing a special view or breaking the rhythm of the façade.

The interior, which carries the black granite exterior base inside as a border, is a series of stunning spaces including an indoor pool and excercise room. The random windows create a sculptural, jazzy ambience inside and the unexpected marble partitions surprise and delight. The living room carpet designed as a giant yellow legal pad (the owner is an attorney) adds a whimsical touch, consistent with the playful atmosphere throughout.

ADDRESS 81 Lakewood Drive, Glencoe
SIZE 7800 square feet (725 square metres)
ROAD I-94 right onto 41, exit Tower Road, follow Sheridan to Lakewood Drive
ACCESS none

Arquitectonica International 1987

Gurnee and Zion

The Power House

This is an interactive museum geared towards teaching the history and uses of energy. The linear building is a simple 336-foot aluminium and steel rectangle with a gabled roof suggestive of local vernacular church architecture. A symbolic temple to energy, the building is elevated on a concrete platform slightly above its parking lot habitat. Liturgical references abound, inspired by both the institution's sacred treatment of energy and the pre-existing religious names of the site boundaries.

Tigerman has written about some of the external forces that formed the building: 'The building's basilica-like form evolves naturally as it is sited at the eastern end of Shiloh Boulevard (the termination of an east–west axis that bisects the Biblically conceived town of Zion ... Additionally, the location of the Zion station is 13-degrees east-south-east from Shiloh Park, putting it into line with Jerusalem, helping to valorise any liturgical connection with the Biblical origins of Zion, which is compounded by each of the four exhibition zones rotating thirteen degrees each)'. This use of the 13-degree angle is apparent in a vaguely deconstructivist increment to the building. Located 200 yards north of the Zion nuclear generating plant, the design responds to it through disjunction. Two emergency fire exits disguised as concrete buttresses and their light steel treillage which also function as brackets for the exhibition hall spear the Power House at 13-degree angles.

Based on a horizontal tripartite plan, the first section conceptually represents a whole that is then deconstructed in the middle area and attempts to be rebuilt unsuccessfully in the final part of the building. This is achieved through the conventional hiding of construction elements in the first section, exaggerating and exposing ductwork, conduits and other structural elements in the midsection (also intended as a symbolic energising or demystifying of the building) and then not fully returning to

Tigerman McCurry 1992

Tigerman McCurry 1992

complete screening of these essentials in the theatre and public rooms at the end of the museum.

This space has then been divided and redivided into eight 42-foot squares which then gain complexity by being diagonally rotated and finally once again orthogonally reconstructed in the same formation as at the entrance.

ADDRESS Shiloh Boulevard, Zion
CLIENT Commonwealth Edison Company
STRUCTURAL ENGINEERS Beer Gorski & Graff
ROAD 294 north to 173 east to Sheridan Road, turn east onto Shiloh, then follow to the lakefront
ACCESS open to the public

Tigerman McCurry 1992

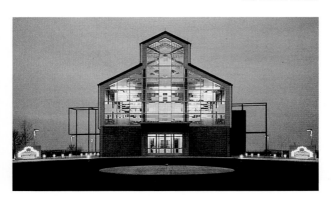

Tigerman McCurry 1992

Illinois Bell Telephone Company, Remote Switching Unit

Slanted white metal pipes and large boulders stand guard over this small brick enclosure. A rectangular box with an off-centre triangular roof balanced on top, the building contains computerised telephone equipment. Programmatically, other than sheltering the apparatus from the weather, this building must do nothing more than properly ventilate the methane gas emitted by telephone cables. An unmanned satellite station, it bears no distinguishing logo or sign.

Although repairmen are the only visitors to this industrial unit, it is seen daily by thousands of shoppers trooping towards the adjacent discount shopping centre. The switching unit is prominently located at the boundary between a large mall and the surrounding horse farms.

The project became a vehicle for exploring the architectural possibilities of representing the idea of machine versus nature. Seven graduated rocks march symbolically across the pavement and lawn towards the building in direct alignment with the northerly pointing roof. This is purely gestural as the boulders serve no function, and sets the contemplative tone of the scheme. Brick, a universal example of technology successfully combined with nature, was chosen as the primary material. Graduated in colour, the shell of the building is intended to appear as though it is rising up out of the ground.

ADDRESS Hunt Club Road at Grand Avenue, Gurnee
CLIENT Illinois Bell Telephone Co., now Ameritech
COST $770,000
STRUCTURAL ENGINEERS Teng and Associates
ACCESS none

Gurnee and Zion

Ross Barney & Jankowski, Inc. 1991

Gurnee and Zion

Ross Barney & Jankowski, Inc. 1991

Index

Chicago: a guide to recent architecture

Chicago: a guide to recent architecture

Chicago: a guide to recent architecture

Index

Chicago: a guide to recent architecture

East 23rd 240
East Walton 104
18th 242
Forest Avenue 284
Grand Avenue 80, 300
Greenview 50
Higgins Road 274
Hunt Club Road 300
Jorie Boulevard 262
Lacey Road 264
Lakewood Drive 292
Madison 186
Michigan Avenue 102, 156
North Canal 84, 206
North Clark 142, 146
North Cleveland Street 40
North Clinton 210
North Dearborn 60, 74, 76, 138, 208
North Desplaines 210
North Lake Shore Drive 62
North LaSalle 146, 170, 182
North Lincoln Avenue 32
North Michigan Avenue 102, 104, 110, 114, 116, 118, 120, 122, 124, 130
North Milwaukee Avenue 280
North Mohawk 42

Streets (continued)
North Orchard 68, 70
North Orleans 36, 54, 208
North Riverside Plaza 204
North Rush 112
North State 80
North Stetson Avenue 134, 136
North Wells 46, 58, 180, 208
Northwest Point Boulevard 278
Park West Avenue 286
Polk 218, 222
Schiller 70
Sheridan Road 290
Shermer Avenue 282
Shiloh Boulevard 296, 298
Solidarity Drive 226
South Canal 218
South Clark 150
South Dearborn 150
South Desplaines 216
South Ellis Avenue 250, 252
South Franklin 190
South La Salle 176
South Lake Shore Drive 226
South LaSalle 166, 178
South Marshfield Avenue 234
South Michigan Avenue 158
South Ravinia Avenue 268
South Shields Avenue 246
South State 162

Photographic
acknowledgements

FRONT COVER Steve Hall, Hedrich-Blessing

SPINE courtesy Bertrand Goldberg Associates, Inc

p 15 Timothy Hursley

p 17 James R. Steinkamp, © Steinkamp/Ballogg Chg.

p 19 Timothy Hursley

p 21 James R. Steinkamp, © Steinkamp/Ballogg Chg.

pp 23, 25 Nick Merrick, Hedrich-Blessing

p 29 Scott McDonald, Hedrich-Blessing

p 31 Hedrich-Blessing, courtesy Murphy/Jahn

p 33 Timothy Hursley

pp 39, 41 © Wayne Cable, Cable Studios

p 45 James R. Steinkamp, © Steinkamp/Ballogg Chg.

p 47 Dan Bakke, courtesy Jordan Mozer & Associates, Ltd

pp 49–51 George Pappageorge

p 55 Paul Warchol

p 57 © George Lambros Photography

p 59 James R. Steinkamp, © Steinkamp/Ballogg Chg.

p 63 Nick Merrick, Hedrich-Blessing

pp 65–67 Bill Hedrich, Hedrich-Blessing

p 69 Mark L. Ballogg, © Steinkamp/Ballogg Chg.

p 75 Howard N. Kaplan, © HNK Architectural Photography, Inc.

p 77 Van Inwegan Photography, Chicago

pp 79, 81 Tillis & Tillis Inc., courtesy Kenzo Tange Associates

p 85 Marco Lorenzetti, Hedrich-Blessing

pp 89, 91 © Wayne Cable, Cable Studios

p 93 Timothy Hursley

p 95 Gregory Murphey

pp 97, 99 © George Lambros Photography

pp 103, 105 Marco Lorenzetti, Hedrich-Blessing

p 107, 109 Sean M. Kinzie, courtesy Hartshorne & Plunkard, Ltd

p 111 © Wayne Cable, Cable Studios

p 113 © Scott Frances/Esto

p 115 Timothy Hursley

p 117 © George Lambros Photography

p 119 Hedrich-Blessing, courtesy Elkus Manfredi Architects Ltd

p 121 courtesy Nike, Inc.

pp 129, 131 courtesy A. Epstein & Sons

p 133 Barbara Karant, Karant + Associates, Inc.

p 135 Gregory Murphey

p 137 Scott McDonald, Hedrich-Blessing

p 139 courtesy Kevin Roche John Dinkeloo & Associates

p 141 Mark L. Ballogg, © Steinkamp/Ballogg Chg.

p 143 Barbara Karant, Karant + Associates, Inc.

pp 145, 147 James R. Steinkamp, © Steinkamp/Ballogg Chg.

pp 149–151 David Clifton

pp 153, 155 courtesy Fujikawa Johnson & Associates, Inc.

p 157 Hedrich-Blessing, courtesy Hammond, Beeby & Babka

p 161 Timothy Hursley

p 163 Judith Bromley

pp 166, 167 Jon Miller, Hedrich–Blessing

p 169 Gregory Murphey

p 171 James R. Steinkamp, © Steinkamp/Ballogg Chg.

p 175 David Clifton

p 181 Nick Merrick, Hedrich-Blessing

p 183 Merrick & McDonald, Hedrich–Blessing

p 187 © Wayne Cable, Cable Studios

p 189 Nick Merrick, Hedrich-Blessing

p 191 Hedrich-Blessing, courtesy Skidmore, Owings & Merrill, Inc.

p 193 © George Lambros Photography

p 195 David Clifton

p 197 Barbara Karant, Karant + Associates, Inc

p 199 Gregory Murphey

pp 201, 203 ©Wayne Cable, Cable Studios

p 205 Nick Merrick, Hedrich-Blessing

p 207 Timothy Hursley

p 211 John Apolinski, courtesy Solomon Cordwell Buenz & Associates

pp 214, 215 Sean M. Kinzie

p 219 © George Lambros Photography

p 221 David Belle

Chicago: a guide to recent architecture

p 223 courtesy Bertrand Goldberg Associates, Inc.
p 225 Nick Merrick, Hedrich-Blessing
pp 228, 229 Chicago Park District
pp 233–235 Steve Hall, Hedrich-Blessing
p 237 Chicago Park District
p 241 Ben Altman
p 243 Samuel Fein
pp 245, 247 courtesy Hellmuth, Obata & Kassabaum, Inc.
p 251 Bob Harr, Hedrich-Blessing
p 253 Bob Shimer, Hedrich-Blessing
pp 257, 259 Barry Rustin, courtesy Ross Barney & Jankowski, Inc.
p 261 Timothy Hursley
p 263 Hedrich-Blessing, courtesy Lohan Associates
p 265 Jon Miller, Hedrich-Blessing
p 267 Barbara Karant, Karant + Associates, Inc.
p 269 Nick Merrick, Hedrich-Blessing
p 273 Steve Hall, Hedrich-Blessing
p 275 James R. Steinkamp, © Steinkamp/Ballogg Chg.
p 277 Nick Merrick, Hedrich-Blessing

p 279 Timothy Hursley
p 281 Howard N. Kaplan © HNK Architectural Photography, Inc.
pp 285, 289, 291 Timothy Hursley
p 293 Tim Street-Porter
pp 297, 299 Van Inwegen Photography, Chicago
p 301 Nick Merrick, Hedrich-Blessing